Comm

# Committed to Peace
## Blue Valley Stake Lecture Series

By Barbara McFarlane Higdon

Herald Publishing House
Independence, Missouri

Herald Publishing House
Independence, Missouri
Printed in the United States of America

Library of Congress Cataloging-in-Publication Data

Higdon, Barbara J.
Committed to Peace : Blue Valley Stake Lectures / by Barbara McFarlane Higdon.
p. cm.
ISBN 0-8309-0679-7
1. Peace—Religious aspects —Christianity. 2. Reorganized Church of Jesus Christ of Latter Day Saints—Doctrines. I. Title. II. Title: Blue Valley Stake Lectures.
BX8643.P43H54 1994
261.8'73—dc20 94-26140
CIP

97 96 95 94 1 2 3 4

# Table of Contents

For Paul, Alex, Kevin, Tim, Dennis,
and all the other grandchildren of this world,
may you live in peace.

# Foreword

The third annual Blue Valley Stake Lecture Series for members of the Central Field was held in the Temple sanctuary in October 1993. Barbara MacFarlane Higdon, director of the Temple Peace Center, spoke on the topic "Committed to Peace." We are pleased that her six lectures are now available in this book, as well as on audiocassettes, through Herald House.

Previous lectures in the series were delivered by President Wallace B. Smith, *The Witness of Reconciliation* (1991), and Apostle Geoffrey F. Spencer, president of the Council of Twelve, *The Promise of Healing* (1992), both published by Herald House. The 1994 lectures will be delivered in the Temple sanctuary by Peter Judd, director of the Temple Worship Center, who will speak on the topic of worship.

We are indebted to many who made the 1993 lectures possible. Joe A. Serig, apostle in charge of the Central Field, continues to give encouragement for the annual lecture series. Presidents of the six Central Field stakes presided at the lectures and assigned assisting ministers. Marci Brown, my administrative assistant, arranged for organists and prepared printed programs for each lecture. Roger Yarrington, who first envisioned the lecture series three years ago, handled publicity and liaison with Electronic Media and Temple staffs. Virgil Bellville headed a competent staff of ushers. Joyce Barnhard and the Blue Valley Stake women's departments provided refreshments each evening.

The exceptional scholarship and presentation by Dr. Higdon were evident to all who attended these lectures. We thank her for adding to our understanding and our commitment to peacemaking.

*Joe D. Donald*
Blue Valley Stake President

# Introduction

These lectures describe a multiplicity of ways individuals and groups attempt to pursue peace. Neither exhaustive nor rigorously critical, this discussion does, however, attempt to present ideas and programs that may hold promise. This panorama of peacemaking thought and effort is part of the heritage and hope of humankind.

A basic assumption of these lectures is that when enough people give priority to the ways of peace, their efforts will diminish the violence present in human experience. A second assumption holds that conflict, which will always characterize human interaction, need not be violent. Between nations, in business and industry, within and between religious faiths, in marriage and family, within ourselves, and in the natural world, conflict is not failure; in fact, it can be creative and developmental. However, when people no longer communicate but seek to coerce each other, conflict becomes nonproductive and alienating.

If peace and conflict are not opposites but exist on a continuum, what then is peace? These lectures offer a number of different definitions, but they do not attempt to describe the non-negotiable minimum conditions that would constitute peace. They do invite the reader to engage in serious, careful thought to identify and discover peaceful ways of living. For the Christian, non-negotiable characteristics and resulting definitions of peace will rise out of his or her understanding of the Christian gospel, an understanding that should be forever growing and changing.

In 1984 the Church of Jesus Christ was explicitly called to pursue peace. The institution has embarked on an exciting journey to discover what it means to pursue peace. An enthusiastic outpouring of creative effort by individuals and many fine worship and study resources produced by the church, only a few of which are described here, have been the response to this prophetic initiative. However, as Martin Marty, distinguished professor of Christian history at the University of Chicago, observed in the *Christian Century* (February 23, 1994) it is too soon to tell where the church will come out as it thinks through what it means to be an institution that pursues peace. In the years ahead, church leadership must develop a coherent set of principles that define that institutional thrust. Is being a church that pursues peace different from being a peace church in the traditional sense of that label? In what ways can a small institution serve as a leaven for peace in a violent world? How does the Church of Jesus Christ become an ensign of peace to the world?

My hope is that these lectures will contribute to a productive dialogue that will go on as long as people of courage and goodwill have breath, and that we will continue to respond, ever more sensitively, to the inspiration of the Divine Spirit.

*Barbara McFarlane Higdon*

# From These Roots a Branch Will Bear Fruit

"All important events in the real world—whether admirable or monstrous—are always spearheaded in the realm of words," writes Vaclav Havel, the recently elected president of the Czech Republic. He knows from his own experience that "words still count for something when you can...go to prison for them." A survivor of a lifetime in a totalitarian state, part of which he spent imprisoned for his words, he continues:

> For forty years now I have read [the word "peace"] on the front of every building and in every shop window in my country. For forty years, an allergy to that beautiful word has been engendered in me as in every one of my fellow citizens because I know what the word has meant here for the past forty years—ever mightier armies ostensibly to defend peace.

Thus Havel reminds us that "in the beginning of everything is the word, the miracle to which we owe the fact that we are human." So much a part of our persona is our language that the way we define a word "reflects the person who utters it, the situation in which it is uttered, and the reason for its utterance."[1] Havel's understanding is especially applicable to our attempts to define "peace." In that effort we reveal our view of reality, our theology, our expectations of ourselves, and our aspirations for the future.

Because the word "peace" has been so badly used for political purposes in recent memory, its rehabilitation is terribly important. Consider the contempt and suspicion the word "peacenik" has carried in our society; or the Communist "doublespeak" to which Havel refers. Or consider the irony—or perhaps even the cynicism—of the motto of the former United States Strategic Air Command: "Peace is our profession." Because of the meanings assigned it, the word "peace" will always reveal personal and societal competition between different values. The continuing effort to define it is worthwhile, however, because it creates as precise a communication as any high-level abstraction ever can. Within the enormous range of meanings, an identification of the most common meanings may build a general consensus or at least a somewhat common basis for discussion of different points of view. And, in the end, we will no doubt discover that, like so many of the ambiguities of human experience, there is no one definition; each of us will need to construct our own as we find our own way to pursue peace.

A superficial look at several ancient words for peace reveals at least four rich traditional perspectives relevant to a definition of peace. From the Semitic tradition of both Jews and Arabs comes an ideal of the unity of all existence. The Hebraic verb *shalem* means "to be complete, to make complete, to finish." *Shalom,* the noun, is a vision of a wholeness of physical world and human society based on a faithful covenant with God, a covenant in which human beings live at an optimal level of existence. *Shalom* as a salutation can also mean "may that which is good within you richly abound." The Arabic salutation *salam* carries a similar meaning. Translated literally it is "peace be unto you." The Slavic word *mir* references both peace and world, suggesting that peace and global wholeness are inextricably joined. *Santi* or *shanti*, the Sanskrit word from which the languages of India take their words for peace, implies an intimate spiritual unity with the cosmos. T.S. Eliot translated it as "the peace that passeth understanding." These definitions have much in common. A somewhat different image is conveyed by the Chinese word *huo'ping* which suggests a balance between opposites (*yin* and *yang*) thus holding in harmony and tranquility a diversity of forces and experiences. In the West still another concept is illustrated in the Greek word *eirene* and the Latin word *pax*. For the ancient Greek, peace was an interlude between wars, part of a predictable historical cycle. However, in the New Testament *eirene* is the word that carries the theme of the Christian message. It describes the new reality created by those who, having overcome their hostility to God, live in a new covenant of love with their fellow human beings. The Roman *pax* referred to an agreement or compact, an imposition of law and order, which included the negative elements caught up in the words pacify, pacification, and even appeasement. These four concepts—the wholeness of individual and society, the equilibrium of opposites, the highly structured political interactions within society, and finally the transformation of human relationships by the transformed individual—provide four approaches to the meaning of peace and give us a rich variety of concepts to inform our contemporary search for useful definitions. [2]

More important for our purposes, however, are the current concepts that determine how those who subscribe to them will define their pursuit of peace. Negative peace refers to the reduction or elimination of organized mass violence. Some scholars who favor this definition believe that to include other elements distracts our attention from the real horror of war and the very real possibility of nuclear annihilation of all life. They believe that, even though war is certainly not the only or even perhaps the most dangerous problem we face, it "most clearly embodies the attitudinal and behavioral barriers to a more humane future and to the functional cooperation needed to create that future."[3] A somewhat broader definition understands peace as the just and nonviolent resolution of conflicts. This definition applies to all levels of human experience from the international to the interpersonal, from the largest institutions to families and individuals.

A limited definition of peace growing from the experience of the United Nations suggests that an achievable ideal of peace and justice would be the result of a society organized in such a way that the felt wants of individuals could be freely expressed; that law, in order to be just, must at least protect that expression and provide it with the channels through which it could compete effectively for (though not necessarily attain) the support of politically organized society. Obviously this does not describe reality even in developed nations. In Second and Third World countries, the mechanisms for its implementation are not yet even in place. This definition, or rather operational description, does have the value of more precision and is perhaps attainable through concrete actions.[4]

Positive peace, on the other hand, envisions a world where justice and personhood prevail, a world governed by compassion and the fulfillment of human needs, developmental as well as physical. This magnificent conception gives us many more words to define—justice, fulfillment, community—words that exist on equally high levels of abstraction. Some scholars have suggested that we can "move towards a transcending consensus by increasing the abstractness of our theoretical models and statements."[5] As much as this view would diminish precision in communication on a rational level, the diversity it stimulates creates an enormous individual creativity that enriches the process of peacemaking.

Another definition sees the absence of violence and the presence of opportunity for human development inseparably connected to a stable, predictable social order, an order that arises from a consensus within a society. A related refinement points out that insistence on order beyond a certain level may actually promote peace*less*ness and *in*justice. Starting from the proposition that the unique individual, not the group, is the basic unit of society, predictable social order seems impossible to attain. Human differences create an infinite variety of behaviors. Noted Norwegian peace scholar, Johan Galtung, postulates that "Associative, high-entropy states remove borders, raise the tolerance for differences, and create a world system of interlocking, positive relationships with a high conflict-absorbing and conflict-solving potential." When needs for basic security are met, people will begin to search for variety, novelty, and change in their lives as they attempt to realize their potential, efforts that produce instability within society. This view implies that after the orderly satisfaction of the basic needs of physical survival, disorderly behavior will be essential for personal development. "Peace is an uninterrupted flow of ordered randomness replicated at every level of human interaction..."; in other words, the apparent oxymoron: "stable chaos."[6] However, for people who have not been blessed with adequate physical necessities, this definition—a noble and humane aspiration—has little applicability.

Some definitions measure peace against the standard of the most deprived people in the world. Working with the Temple Peace Center Advisory Committee, Rod Downing offered a definition that describes peace as "the well-being of all life within the functioning support of nature, measured by its effects on the most disadvantaged."[7] Thus attention shifts from the problems of organized violence to individual physical deprivation and economic development, to environment and resources, to universal human rights and social justice.

Shifting emphasis from external to internal states, peace, pursued primarily through religious discipline, is found not in the minds of people but in their souls, as the preamble to the UNESCO Charter proclaims. Unconditional love offered by one individual to other individuals grows from this personal state and is transformed into social and global action. To some Western minds, until the human heart is changed, no other forms of peace can be realistically pursued. To others, concrete action is the only meaningful way peace can be pursued. Thus Marxists are not alone in ignoring the spiritual reality of life, postulating that justice and prosperity for all can be achieved through social engineering. A holistic approach would include both personal transformation and refinement of social structures, integrating the individual and the social and political.[8] The United Methodist Church proclaims:

> Peace is not simply the absence of war, a nuclear stalemate or combination of uneasy cease-fires. It is that emerging dynamic reality envisioned by prophets where spears and swords give way to implements of peace; where historic antagonists dwell together in trust; and where righteousness and justice prevail. There will be no peace with justice until unselfish and informed love are structured into political processes and international arrangements.[9]

Acknowledging the impact of political activity on the process of achieving a just and equitable society, peace can be seen, then, as not so much a state of being as a maintenance of the balance between the individual and society through perpetual adjustments. The question posed earlier, "What is peace?" may be the wrong one to ask. The peace described by many of these definitions is active effort. We need a new word, a verb perhaps, to convey process rather than state. Gandhi observed: "There is no way to peace; peace is the way."[10]

The religious and ethical traditions and attitudes of the world's great religions toward war and peace contribute to the search for definitions of peace. Characterized by ambiguity of principle vis-à-vis practice, their theologies offer resources for both war and peace. Containing beautiful visions of peace, many religious traditions have inspired or supported war. Religious values are powerful influences on human behavior, so powerful in fact that Hans Küng, a distinguished Swiss theologian, has suggested: "There can be no peace among the nations without peace among the religions. There can be no peace among the religions without dialogue between the religions. There can be no dialogue between the religions without research into their theological foundations."[11]

Responding to that challenge, the following very brief and extremely superficial examination of five of the six major world religious traditions identifies some of the resources for peace within them and attempts to describe their vision of what peace should be. These generalizations cannot describe the diversity of thought found within each faith, differences at least as great as between the traditions themselves. This analysis attempts only to identify significant differences in beliefs and worldviews and to discover common ground. We should celebrate both the valuable insights that are not part of our own tradition and those beliefs and values held in common.

The tolerance and respect recommended by Paul—"Do you suppose God is the God of the Jews alone? Is he not the God of the Gentiles also? Certainly, of Gentiles also, if it be true that God is one" (Romans 3:29–30)—are also found in the Book of Mormon:

> Know ye not that there are more nations than one? Know ye not that I, the Lord your God, have created all men....And because I have spoken one word, ye need not suppose that I cannot speak another;...Wherefore, because ye have a bible, ye need not suppose that it contains all my words; neither need ye suppose that I have not caused more to be written....For out of the books which shall be written, I will judge the world, every man according to his works, according to that which is written.—II Nephi 12:55–56, 63–64, 66

With that validation, we encounter the richness and the fallibility of five major world religions. We discover common themes described in the words of James Adams as "outgoing love engendering an open, ecumenical community creatively concerned with social justice, a community in which mutual acceptance and common responsibility are the touchstones."[12]

Understandings of human/divine interaction differ widely. For example, two of the three Semitic religions, Judaism and Islam, within their prophetic traditions describe continual confrontation between God and human beings. God's justice is highest priority. The Indian religions, Buddhism and Hinduism, are more inward, mystical, and nonindividualistic. Confucianism and other Chinese traditions offer advice for achieving harmonious balance in this life. All three Eastern religions believe that the development of individual spiritual maturity is the foundation for peace; that personal discipline is desirable and is achieved in Hinduism through yoga, in Buddhism through meditation, and in Confucianism through study. All five would agree that a person's duty to society is more important than the service that society renders the individual.[13]

These religious traditions also hold in common a concept of holy war. Ancient Hebraic and Islamic traditions view sacred warfare as the means of reestablishing a right relationship between people and their god and as a corrective for history run amok. James Aho calls this a transcendent-historical holy war. In the Eastern faiths holy war is an antidote to a disruption of cosmological order. God's pervading Spirit has been challenged and human beings must put down that challenge. This is the immanentist-cosmological myth. Many of history's religiously motivated conflicts, however, have been inspired by the desire to preserve the status quo or expand influence and a particular way of life. They have invoked their sacred tradition for support and validation.[14]

Side by side with these similarities stand provocative differences. Buddha, for example, by renouncing all material pleasures achieved simplicity, nonviolence, diligence, and compassion. Having simplified his existence, he was freed of human distractions to search for truth. After learning to control and subdue his response to external stimuli, he turned his attention to his own body and learned to control its functions. His existence was thus liberated from greed, hatred, and illusion. He had attained the highest perfection. This way of life, the Middle Path, is available to anyone who would submit to its discipline. It creates a peaceful, positive, nonviolent life. In pure Buddhism violence is only justified in defense of the homeland. At the heart of Buddhist life are the five ethical precepts expected of all believers: to not kill, not lie, not steal, not commit unchaste acts, and not take intoxicants. The Buddhist sees peace first of all as a spiritual state that acknowledges that good effects cannot come from bad intentions or actions. Thus it is not possible in the Buddhist scheme of things to believe that if a nation wants peace it should prepare for war. The concept of Nirvana suggests "supreme peace." The opposite of peace is seen as suffering, and the task of the Buddhist is to identify the causes of that suffering. Greed arises from the misconception that the things of this world, including oneself, are permanent and therefore possessable. Acquired through meditation, the attributes of sympathy, compassion, loving-kindness, and self-discipline move a person toward Nirvana. Anger, conflict, and violence are to be rooted out of behavior. "Do not kill a living being, You should not kill or condone killing by others, Having abandoned the use of violence you should not use force against either the strong or the feeble." [15] Not only do these principles prohibit the participation of a Buddhist in war (except for defense of the homeland) they also describe the Buddhist ideal of interpersonal and community interaction.

Buddhist scripture places high value on human relationships. Community values supersede individualistic ones in the faithful Buddhist society. At the same time the democratic practices of group decision making and individual participation are part of Buddha's teaching. This strong sense of community accounts for one of the historic strengths of Buddhism: its adaptability. It has frequently found a place in many different social and political systems. Employing pacifist methods, Buddhists participated in the effort to achieve independence from the British in Burma and Sri Lanka. The nonviolent tradition adapted to political purposes was unforgettably demonstrated in the self-immolation of monks in Vietnam in 1963. The Soka Gakkai, the third most powerful political party in Japan today, was inspired to a degree by Buddhism and has consistently opposed the nuclear arms race. The adaptability of Buddhism, however, did not extend to cooperation with the Chinese communists who attempted, with little success, to attract Buddhists to their revolutionary struggle by invoking carefully selected and interpreted scriptural passages. "Buddhism has primarily influenced the societies it has permeated in a positive and peaceful direction...."[16] However, the ritual combat, the *do*, has been used for violent purposes such as fanatical participation in war.[17]

Two passages from Buddhist scriptures illustrate the spirit of the faith:

> A man finds no justice if he carries a dispute to violence. No, he who knows right from wrong, who is learned and

guides others—not by violence, but by the same law, being a guardian of the law, who shows intelligence: he is called just.[18]

> To dwell in a peaceful land, with right desires in one's heart—This is the greatest blessing. Control of self and peaceful speech, and whatever word be well spoken—This is the greatest blessing. To live righteously, to give help to kindred, to follow a peaceful calling—This is the greatest blessing.[19]

Confucius and his followers believe that people's hearts can be changed. Social transformation would then follow that spiritual transformation. In the *Analects, li* or ritual correctness is the highest value standing above *yi*, moral rightness, and *fa*, legal justice.[20] The following passage from the Words of Confucius describes a close chain of cause and effect—action and reaction. It explains the process by which peaceful order comes into being:

> The ancients, when they wished to exemplify illustrious virtue throughout the empire, first brought peace and order to their states. Desiring to bring peace and order to their states, they first brought the same to their families. Wishing to bring peace to their families, they first cultivated themselves. Wishing to cultivate themselves, they first purified their purposes. Wishing to purify their purposes, they first sought to think sincerely. Wishing to think sincerely, they first extended their knowledge as widely as possible. They did this by the investigation of all things. By investigation of things, their knowledge became extensive; their knowledge being extensive, their thoughts became sincere; their thoughts being sincere, their purposes were rectified; their purposes being rectified, they cultivated themselves; having cultivated themselves, their families were regulated; their families having been regulated, their states were governed rightly; their states being rightly governed, the empire was thereby brought to peace and prosperity.[21]

The karma of Hinduism is a moral law of cause and effect. Whether seen as a process involving many generations or within one lifetime, what people do in the present determines what will happen in the future, just as what has been done in the past determines the present. Arjuna, the protagonist of the Bhagavad-Gita, the Hindu war epoch, expressing his dilemma about war, echoes the concerns of all thoughtful people. Warfare, condemned in the Gita, is the effect of human failure, the greatest wrong choice that people can make. Because the world is just, each act that contravenes that justice requires compensatory suffering, which often takes the form of war.[22] Gandhi interpreted the Bhagavad Gita as an allegory, not about war at all, but about the human spirit pursuing its goal.[23] The Gita defines a peaceful ethic and the mechanism for its realization: "If you want to see the brave, look at those who can forgive. If you want to see the heroic, look at those who can love in return for hatred."[24]

The Hindus have a legend concerning a mythical bird called Bherunda. The bird has a single body, but two necks, two heads, and two separate consciences. After an eternity together, these two heads begin to hate each other and decide to do harm to each other. Both of them swallow pebbles and poison with the result that the whole Bherunda bird goes into spasms and dies with loud cries of pain. It is brought back to life by the infinite mercy of Krishna, to remind people that hatred harms not only the object of that hatred, but at the same time, and perhaps chiefly, the one who hates.[25] We do not have to look any further to find the inspiration for the ethic of the passive resistance movement led by Gandhi.

For the Muslim, Allah is the all-holy, the all-peace. Important political and social practices and beliefs regarding peace and human rights characterize Islamic tradition. Based on the Koran and the Sunnah (the practices of the Prophet Muhammad), the Islamic imperative is to establish a just social order containing rights and duties to Allah and to Allah's creatures. The creation and administration of just laws is required of the political system. Also central to the Islamic message is the cultivation of love and respect for the natural world and kindness and compassion for all of humankind. Supported by this ethic, then, peace emerges from the justice created by the power of the political system. People expect government to provide for their needs and to help them become self-sufficient. The system, in return, expects the individual to make no unreasonable demands on it. This ethic emphasizes community rather than individual freedom, except as individuals choose to follow the will of Allah. Important to note in light of the Islamic fundamentalism that has had so much recent attention, Islam has in the past fostered unusual tolerance for cultural pluralism. This characteristic is both the cause and effect of its historic ethnic diversity. However, when nationalism replaces cultural pluralism, precious tolerance is lost, and the outside world overgeneralizes about the rigidity of Islamic values.[26]

The excesses of Islamic fundamentalism are deplorable as excesses always are in any ideology. These fundamentalist sects have capitalized on the wretched conditions of the poor, finding strong support through their willingness to create a community for and of the dispossessed people of the Middle East. Their leaders were not elected by democratic processes to represent the group, and they have, without doubt, exploited the appalling conditions of daily life of what seems to have become a permanent refugee community. The Islamic world faces a great challenge in preserving and applying the great Islamic traditions of justice, truth, and good works to the changing conditions of modern life. To understand that is to begin to understand the ferment within predominantly Muslim countries today.[27]

The attitude toward change that has characterized Islamic tradition presents important insights into the Islamic worldview. Rejecting historic determinism, the Muslim sees change as intentionally brought about by individuals, who then bear responsibility for its consequences. The jihad or holy war has been for many Muslims over the centuries a powerful agent for change. Some traditions justified it only when the unbelievers were the aggressors.[28] Change is also internal and can occur in the hearts and souls of individuals. Speaking to the 1993 RLDS Peace Colloquy, Riffat Hassan described the teaching of the Koran concerning the "greater *jihad*," a struggle against one's own arrogance and the "lesser *jihad*," a struggle against external things that obstruct one's approach to God.

The Islamic worldview sees life as a web of interconnectedness presided over by a God who reigns over all creation. All believers are equal and are called upon to offer compassion to the poor. Ramadan, one of the most sacred observances of the Muslim year, requires a daily fast, the purpose of which is to demonstrate solidarity with the hungry.

The Muslim believes that the Koran contains divine revelation in its pure form and provides a code of conduct for all people. God is revealed through a succession of prophets of which Jesus is one. When enough people purify themselves, the laws of God will be established on earth. Peace comes when human beings surrender their will to God's will. The words of Muhammed repeatedly emphasize its attainability,

> All of God's creatures belong to the family of God. The person most beloved of God, therefore, is he or she who does real good to the members of God's family.[29]

And in another passage,

> Shall I not tell you what is better than prayers and fasting and giving alms to the poor? It is making peace between one another: enmity and malice destroy all virtues.[30]

And in another passage,

> A man said to the Prophet, "Give me a command." He said, "Let nothing provoke thee to anger." The man said to the Prophet, "Give another command." And he replied, "Let nothing provoke thee to anger." The man repeated the question several times and the Prophet said, "Let nothing provoke thee to anger."[31]

In 1977 Anwar Sadat, the president of Egypt and a devout Muslim, addressed the Knesset in Jerusalem in that historic peacemaking act that cost him his life. On that occasion he offered a contemporary affirmation of these basic Islamic principles: "God's teaching and commandments are love, sincerity, security and peace."

Because we inherit the Judeo-Christian tradition, we in the West need to understand our roots and to identify and evaluate the influence this past had had on our behavior both as individuals and societies. Our inheritance from the Old Testament contains, as do the traditions already examined, a wide variety of contradictory ideas about peace which have not remained static over the centuries. For example, the phrase "from these roots a branch will bear fruit" comes from the eleventh Chapter of Isaiah and opens the beautiful description of the peaceable kingdom. Written at a time of internal crisis for Israel, it affirms that "God's promises will prevail in, with, and through geopolitical reality."[32] Like Islam, Judaism believes that social justice is a high ideal superseding any other form of relationship between human beings. From a legalistic "eye for an eye" letter-of-the-law interpretation, the concept of Hebraic justice evolved toward a generous and compassionate ideal. As we have already seen, the concept of *shalom* articulates a magnificent ethic of relationship between justice and peace in which personal peace joins with the social peace of nations (Micah 4:3–4). Believed to be an important attribute of God's intention for creation, social justice requires concrete action. This principle mandates compassion for one's enemies (Proverbs 25:21). People need to develop habits of charity, generosity, and concern to put the good times of life in proper perspective, and to help them through the bad times with grace. This behavior is seen as emulating God's covenant with Israel, which provides the model.[33] Even though this high ethical ideal is repeatedly expressed, the Old Testament is a book about war. The brutality and bloodshed of the Israelites, from interpersonal behavior to national conquest, provides a jarring contradiction to the ethical teaching about peace and justice. The narrative implies that it is only through the establishment, by the sword if necessary, of the lordship of God over all nations that divine peace will come to this world. The Old Testament repeatedly celebrates unrestrained "holy war" in which Yahweh himself serves as the commanding general.

Along with these human rationalizations for conquest and failure of individual relationships, however, stands the great vision of peace and justice that has kept alive the ancient hope for a just and peaceful world. The great biblical metaphors have created powerful symbols that inspire Western culture, whether or not individuals accept them as inspired scripture. The lion, lamb, and the little child, the beating of swords into plowshares, and the living waters of justice give concrete expression to the meaning of peace.

Faithful to their Old Testament foundations, the Torah and the Talmud also give voice to the highest expressions of this dream: "More knowledge, more life. More justice, more peace."[34] "Great is peace, for it is equal to everything."[35] "Great is peace, because if the Jews were to practice idolatry, and peace prevailed among them at the same time, God would say, 'I cannot punish them, because peace prevails among them.' "[36] The traditional "Song of Peace" summarizes the role of peace in human affairs and its relationship to God:

> Grant us peace, Thy most precious gift, O Thou eternal source of peace, and enable Israel to be its messenger unto the peoples of this earth. Strengthen the bonds of friendship and fellowship among the inhabitants of all lands. Plant virtue in every soul and may the love of Thy name hallow every heart. Praised be thou, O Lord, our God, giver of peace.[37]

Memorable words invoking the great Jewish tradition of peace concluded the remarks of Yitzhak Rabin when he spoke on the south lawn of the White House during the signing of the accords between Israel and the PLO in August 1993, words uttered at the end of the daily Jewish prayer: "Peace be to them that are far off and to them that are near."

A discussion of the beliefs and values of the religions that have shaped the worldview and behavior of enormous numbers of the world's peoples suggests some promising opportunities for the pursuit of peace. Religion speaks of ultimates—the ultimate concerns of human beings and, however imperfectly envisioned, an Ultimate Being. It does not matter what name we give that being. An ethical tension should always exist between that being and the world, because religious truth should judge contemporary society, challenging all human assumptions and behavior. Our best understanding of prophetic truth compels us to engage in a rigorous examination of our individual lives and of our society.

Religion is not science; religion is not politics. These differences can provide a framework for the contribution that a dialogue among the world's great religions can make to the pursuit of peace. The religious method stands in contrast to the modern belief that real truth can be apprehended only through the scientific method: only that which can be seen, measured, or weighed is real. This method has been responsible for tremendous and positive human achievement, but it has not solved all human problems. Indeed, it has created a whole host of new ones. The dual goals of science—understanding and mastery of the environment and the creation of greater human comfort—are responsible for many of them. A distinction between politics and religion is also instructive. Politics uses external power to exert direct control on human beings. The fallibility of leaders and the shortsightedness of national interest are tremendously dangerous. Religion inspires and motivates people through the power of great symbols to place the interests of other people and of the human community ahead of their own. Religious leaders interpret the old symbols for a given time or create new ones from the resources of the past—new wine in old bottles.

Every religious tradition has its origin in a historical setting and has been influenced by it. Growing out of these historical particularities are significant differences, some deeply conflicting. However, at their highest levels of abstraction, similarities, even convergence, can be found. For example, all of the religious traditions described here emphasize interpersonal relationships over radical individualism and material acquisition. These ideals, rather than the contemporary Western secular confidence in material things, create the environment for genuine community founded on love and compassion. Thus even in the midst of diversity, a sense of solidarity among the world's great religions can come into being. Could it be that it is in these convergences, as we come to understand them better, we will discover a timeless divine voice trying, by emphasis and repetition, to be heard above the noise of our own history and culture?

In their finest moments, the great religions of the world have proclaimed peace to their own faithful when they have supported oppression and to political powers when they have waged war. "Communities of faith are obligated by their belief in a loving God of justice and mercy to stand against any worldly power that threatens the peace and wellbeing of individuals or community." The world's religions remind politicians of the sanctity of life, the value of community, the dignity of the individual.[38]

Hans Küng notes that the religions of the world hold an authority different from other worldly organizations, an authority that emphasizes morality in human relationships. In this commonality he sees the possibility of an ecumenism among the world's great religions based not on what divides them, but on common beliefs that could bring them together. He notes some striking ethical similarities among them: do not kill; do not lie; do not steal; do not practice immorality; do respect parents and love children. He cites the existence of a "golden rule" that upholds a fundamental ethical principle of human relationships. The Kyoto Conference on Religion and Peace, held in 1973, identified the following commonalities:

> a conviction of the fundamental unity of the human family, of the equality and dignity of all human beings; a sense of the sacredness of the individual person and his conscience; a sense of the value of the human community; a recognition that might is not right, that human power is not self-sufficient and absolute; a belief that love,compassion, unselfishness and the force of inner truthfulness and of the spirit have ultimately greater power than hate, enmity and self-interest; a sense of obligation to stand on the side of the poor and the oppressed as against the rich and the oppressors; a profound hope that good will finally prevail.[39]

Küng emphasizes, however, that any ecumenism must acknowledge that all beliefs are not of equal value, and that orthodoxy should not be viewed as the final criterion for human salvation or damnation and should not seek to impose its claim to truth by means of force. He recommends that the faithful adherent of any tradition make a careful distinction between the view from the outside and the view from within. This perspective demands holding an uneasy tension between loyalty to personal belief and an openness to the beliefs of others. No believer, then, abandons adherence to the unique message of his or her own faith nor gives up the inspired status of the founder or prophet, but does at the same time confess that the content of the faith is dependent on historical and cultural experience. Most important, all believers need to engage in a critical search for the true and the false within their own faith. Küng suggests criteria for that critique: an ethical criterion requires that religion should not suppress and destroy humanity, but should protect and further it; a religious criterion requires that each faith be true to its own origin or canon, to its authentic "nature," its normative scripture or figure. Finally, the criterion for Christians requires faithfulness to the Spirit of Jesus Christ in theology and practice. Furthermore, belief in one's own religion as true in no way excludes truth in other religions and can allow them their own validity. Küng reminds us that "Dialogue and witness do not exclude each other."[40]

Any attempt to define peace will raise more questions than it answers. Attempting to do so, however, can inform the search of each of us for ways that we may be peacemakers. Is it possible to define peace in such clear, robust ways that the pursuit of peace will contain the excitement, vigor, stress, and turmoil, and produce the dedication that has heretofore made war so appealing? Can human beings create a global ecumenism among the world's great religions and the various factions within them, based on the pursuit of peace? Can they maintain cherished differences yet establish common, but challenging ethical principles and a belief in a transcendent reality to inspire us?

From these roots, may many branches bear blessed fruit.

## Notes

1. Vaclav Havel, "Word on Words," *The New York Review of Books* (July 1989): 8.
2. Vincent Kavaloski, "Pax Romana," *Viewpoints* l, no. 1: 34–39; John Macquarrie, *The Concept of Peace, The Firth Lectures* (Philadelphia: Trinity Press International, 1973), 14–16; and Ulrich Mauser, *The Gospel of Peace: A Scriptural Message for Today's World* (Louisville, Kentucky: Westminster/John Knox Press, 1992), 170–172.
3. Robert Pickus, quoted in *Approaches to Peace: An Intellectual Map*, W. Scott Thompson and Kenneth Jensen, eds. (United States Institute of Peace), 230–231.
4. Julius Stone, *Vision of World Order: Between State Power and Human Justice* (Baltimore, Maryland: Johns Hopkins University Press, 1984), 71.
5. Quoted by Ira Chernus, "Order and Disorder in the Definition of Peace," *Peace & Change: A Journal of Peace Research* 18, no. 2 (April 1993): 111.
6. Ibid., 113.
7. Rod Downing, letter to Wayne Ham (June 6, 1991).
8. John Macquarrie, 2–3.
9. *The Peace Bible*, Steven Scholl, ed. (Los Angeles: Kalimat Press, 1986), 68.
10. Quoted by Betty A. Reardon, *Comprehensive Peace Education: Educating for Global Responsibility* (New York: Teachers College, Columbia University, 1988), 16.
11. Hans Küng, *Global Responsibility: In Search of a New World Ethic* (New York: Crossroad Press, 1991), 104–105.
12. James Adams, "World Religions' Contribution to Peace," *Christian Century* (October 24, 1979): 1040–1043.
13. Denise Carmody and John Carmody, *Peace and Justice in the Scriptures of the World Religions* (New York: Paulist Press, 1988), 78.
14. James A. Aho, *Religious Mythology and the Art of War: Comparative Religious Symbolisms of Military Violence* (Westport, Connecticut: Greenwood Press, 1981), 11.
15. Stewart McFarlane, "Buddhism," *World Encyclopedia of Peace*, Volume 1 (Oxford: Pergamon Press, 1986), 97–103.
16. Ibid.
17. James A. Aho, 138 and 224.
18. Steven Scholl, 28.
19. Ibid., 2.
20. Carmody and Carmody, 70–95.
21. Steven Scholl, 37–38.

22. Thomas Keefe and Ron E. Roberts, *Realizing Peace: An Introduction to Peace Studies* (Ames, Iowa: Iowa State University Press, 1991), 84.
23. Stewart McFarlane, 102.
24. Steven Scholl, 23.
25. Abdul Aziz Said, "The Islamic Context for Human Rights," *Breakthrough* 10, no. 2–3, (Winter/Spring, 1989): 39–41; Elie Wiezel, "The Anatomy of Hate: Resolving Conflict Through Dialogue and Democracy," *Foundation for Humanity*, (August 29, 1990): 20.
26. Keefe and Roberts, 82–83.
27. Ibid.
28. Ibid.
29. Steven Scholl, 101.
30. Ibid., 35
31. Ibid., 32–33.
32. Walter Brueggemann, "Powered By The Spirit," *Sojourners* (May 1991): 11–15.
33. Douglas J. Harris, *Shalom* (Grand Rapids, Michigan: Baker Book House, 1970), 35.
34. Steven Scholl, 61.
35. Carmody and Carmody, 134.
36. John Ferguson, "The Peace Tradition in Judaism: The Talmud" in *War and Peace in the World's Religions* (London: Oxford University Press, 1977), 86–96.
37. Steven Scholl, 99.
38. Ibid., xiii.
39. Hans Küng, 1–103.
40. Ibid.

# In Search of a New Tradition

All of us for whom religion is important engage in theological activity. We experience an inner life of devotion; we engage in serious rational thought about the relationship between ultimate and finite matters; and we hold a life of service as an ideal. All three activities—devotion, thought, and service—take place within the framework of our understanding of the relationship of the Christian gospel to our existence. An intense human need to find significance for human life drives this process. For Christians, divine revelation in history—the incarnation of God in Christ— provides the basis for this understanding, even though we will always imperfectly understand it.

The substance of our theology comes from at least two sources—the wisdom of the past and the experience of the present. What does the wisdom of the past tell us, as Christians, about peace? We have already briefly reviewed the ideals of peace and justice that are fundamental in Judaism. Building on that ethical foundation, Christ's life models a very demanding standard of conduct in that peace and justice play a central role. In both vision and practice, the Christian story proclaims this centrality. The song of the angels at the birth of

Christ; the Sermon on the Mount; the parable of the Good Samaritan; the unresisted arrest and death—all proclaim the "Gospel of Peace." Much of the New Testament resonates with joy and triumph in response to the good news of this gospel. The very repetition of the phrase "the God of Peace" suggests that in the word "peace" some New Testament authors, especially Paul, found an appropriate vehicle to carry the whole content of the Christian gospel.

Ulrich Mauser has noted that, "The task of bringing peace to earth is so essential to the accomplishment of the mission of Christ that a neglect of this aspect would lead to a complete misconstrual of Jesus' persona and work." James 2:15–16 (NRSV) enhances the definition of peace by affirming the importance of the physical necessities of life to a condition of peace. Not only did Jesus heal the spirit but he also ministered to the physical needs of his community. "[T]he entire activity of Jesus, of word and deed, is the making of peace; and...the life of this community is given direction by his blessing on the peacemakers." The three sayings found in Matthew 5:39–41 (NRSV), which deal with response to personal injustice and provocation, describe an ultimate act of peacemaking. Recommended is a positive response to initial injury, which has the possibility of breaking the reciprocal chain of heaping injury upon injury. "Grace and peace," is not an empty formula but brings together the divine act of reconciliation and the blessing of peace. This exemplifies a new form of humanness radically different from anything that had come before. A global peace is also envisioned. Christ is our peace because he has created a new reality and order for human community. The Christian evangel clearly identifies the Holy Spirit as the source of peace and reconciliation.[1]

Christians cannot escape the work of peacemaking, called as we are to mobilize the spirit of peace in behalf of truth and justice in the world (John 20:21 and Luke 24:36). Joy, reconciliation, and peace should define our personal behavior as we seek to follow the teachings of Jesus. His death and resurrection proclaim that love can overcome the demonic forces of violence and hatred. Not only that, but the cross calls us to participate in solidarity with the poor and the oppressed, sharing their pain and suffering. Christ's example calls us to be spiritual centers for relationships in community. We recognize the divine image in ourselves as the basis for our peaceful relationship with the whole world.[2] This covenantal relationship between us and all of God's creation makes us the children of God through our role as peacemakers, as the Sermon on the Mount promises. As peacemakers we should attempt to balance peace with justice, liberation with reconciliation, personal freedom with social equality.[3] Personal integrity and responsible participation in community constitute the wholeness that is the human response to the covenantal relationship with God. All relationships, so understood, become sacramental. God invites us to participate in the ongoing process of creation by participating in the process of peacemaking in this world.

Human beings often do not work to reshape the world according to their best understanding of God's intention for it. In addition to an all-too-common slothfulness, we fail to do so for at least two reasons: the first is that we believe God will provide solutions; the second is our belief that God does not intend for some problems to be solved before the end of time. This apocalyptic belief has allowed us to tolerate injustice and evil in the world, believing in all sincerity in a cosmic division of labor. To be sure, peace belongs to God, and perfect peace is impossible in this world. But this reality does not excuse us from pursuing peace with all our strength. Respecting our freedom, God does not solve our problems for us, but sustains us as we take responsibility as cocreators with God in the work of creation.

The wisdom of the past does indeed inform the present. But that is not our only theological resource. The experience of the present also provides the raw material for our theology of peace. For example, environmental issues and nuclear power are two powerful experiences of our day that are defined by certain theological assumptions. Acting on the belief that the covenant with God embraces all the created world, we need to confess that our environmental crisis developed from a misconception concerning the relationship between nature and human beings. Unlike the Hindu-Buddhist reverence for nature, the Judeo-Christian-Muslim attitude views the natural world as a force to be broken to our will.

Huston Smith offers as example a clear contrast between Eastern and Western points of view: "When Mount Everest was scaled the phrase commonly used in the West to describe the feat was 'the conquest of Everest.' " An Oriental...[philosopher whose thought has] been deeply influenced by Taoism remarked, "We would put the matter differently. We would speak of 'the befriending of Everest.' "[4] Descartes spoke of the role of science "to make us master and possessors of nature," and Francis Bacon's goal was "to bend all nature into the service of man." Carl Sagan notes that both Western religion and Western science have maintained that nature should not be viewed as sacred. This belief has fueled the effort in Western society to exploit nature for physical comfort and economic advantage and is partly responsible for the worldwide environmental crisis we face. Equally culpable, of course, are the incompetent technologies and massive disregard for human welfare in the former Communist bloc that have resulted in enormous pollution and nuclear contamination and the desperate exploitation of nature for economic benefit in Third World countries. Pope John Paul II suggested a proper balance between science and religion when he wrote: "Science can purify religion from error and superstition; religion can purify science from idolatry and false absolutes. Each can draw the other into a wider world, a world in which both can flourish....Such bridging ministries must be nurtured and encouraged."[5]

In the summer of 1993 I visited Kiev, Ukraine, and was privileged to tour the Chernobyl Museum, dedicated to the heroic firefighters who gave their lives in the first hours and days following the nuclear accident. The personal possessions of the dispossessed families spoke in mute eloquence of the emotional cost. Hanging above the interior stairway up which visitors approached the museum proper were fifty oblong road markers, each with the name of one of the affected villages. Through each sign ran the red slash that indicates that the traveler is leaving that village, a poignant and silent testament to the effects of a peacetime nuclear disaster.

Despite the enormous problems that exist, a determination to improve the earth's environment has come into being. The Global Forum of Spiritual and Parliamentary Leaders, held in April 1988, attracted people from nearly 100 nations. Hundreds of spiritual leaders from eighty-three countries and thirty-seven national and international religious bodies have signed the "Scientists' Appeal on the Environment." Among the signatories are the World Muslim League; the World Council of Churches; the World Jewish Congress; the Catholics of All Armenias; grand muftis from Syria and the former Yugoslavia; the Metropolitan Pitrim of Russia; the presiding bishops of all the Christian Churches of China; representatives of Episcopal, Lutheran, Methodist, and Mennonite churches in the United States; and fifty cardinals, lamas, archbishops, head rabbis, patriarchs, mullahs, and bishops of major world cities.[6] The Bruntland Report, commissioned by the United Nations, and the resulting Earth Summit Conference held in Rio de Janeiro in 1992 are unprecedented responses to the urgent need for environmental reform. Madam Gro Bruntland has written: "The development of the Earth to provide a basic level of comfort for all humanity and the protection of the global environment are two sides of the single coin of human survival."[7] By lobbying, marching, recycling, and boycotting, thousands of people are making the healing of the environment a common cause, motivated by a concept of stewardship whose origins can be found theologically in the covenant between human beings and God that includes all aspects of creation.

A second defining experience of our day is the existence of nuclear power. Gordon Kaufman suggests that the atomic age presents us with an unprecedented historical and religious challenge, which he describes as "the logical tension between the traditional view of God's sovereignty and the destructive power which now appears to rest unequivocally in human hands...." Traditional theology has always viewed the endtime as

God's initiative, a final decisive victory over evil. With the unleashing of the power of the atom, humankind has assumed that initiative. Nuclear war can end the achievements of the long, slow process of the creation of all life on Earth. From primordial slime to sentient life, human beings acquired the ability to talk and think, to image and create. The human ability to think about love, truth, freedom, peace, and justice is the creative grace of God at work within us.[8] Some Christians believe God has willed or even directed the scientific developments that have harnessed nuclear power. Others believe God will never allow nuclear destruction to occur and that for that reason we have been safe for the forty years of the arms race.

If we believe in a God who has given us agency, we cannot accept either of these positions. Is it possible to find any redeeming value in the monstrous stockpiles of destructive nuclear weapons or in the damnable worldwide trafficking in weapons, made even more dangerous by the breakup of the Soviet Union? (As recently as the fall of 1993, the Chinese began nuclear testing again, and there is every reason to believe the North Koreans have developed nuclear weapons.) Can the present situation be viewed as anything but a potential disaster for God as well as for humankind? If widespread use of nuclear weapons should occur, human beings will bear responsibility for bringing the curtain down on God's creation. Jonathan Schell leaves little doubt that the loss of life, the poisoning of the environment, and the subsequent nuclear winter will destroy almost if not all life on earth. For the first time in human history, we face the possibility that a generation yet unborn will have no future. He writes:

> Death cuts off life; extinction cuts off birth. Death dispatches into the nothingness after life each person who has been born; extinction in one stroke locked up in the nothingness before life all the people who have not yet been born. For we are finite beings at both ends of our existence—natal as well as mortal—and it is in the nationality of our kind that extinction threatens. We have always been able to send people to their death, but only now has it become possible to prevent all birth and so doom all future human beings to un-creation.[9]

Some theologians have seen our present position as the ultimate rebellion of human beings against God. We have taken over the role of creator. Robert Oppenheimer must have understood that when he quoted the words of Krishna from the Bhagavad-Gita in the moments following the first atomic test explosion at Alamogordo, New Mexico, in 1945; "I am become Death, the shatterer of worlds."

If we have usurped the role of God, we must then be accountable for the future of humanity in a way unprecedented in human history. Two statements that evoke the great Christian symbol of the star of Bethlehem, a universal symbol of peace, express in unforgettable counterpoint that choice. Henry Nelson Wieman writes:

> The bomb that fell on Hiroshima cut history in two like a knife. Before and after are two different worlds. That cut is more abrupt, decisive, and revolutionary than the cut made by the star over Bethlehem....It is more swiftly transformative of human existence than anything else that has ever happened. The economic and political order fitted to the age before that parachute fell becomes suicidal in the age coming after. The same breach extends into education and religion.[10]

Juxtapose that statement with one that contains a blasphemous arrogance: "We want permanent peace.

Let us follow the light that can lead us to it....Since the stars gave us the hydrogen bomb, we can call it the saving Star of Bethlehem."[11]

This second statement gives foundation to G. Clarke Chapman's accusation that nuclearism deserves to be called a Christian heresy. He charges that the implications flowing from the assumptions held by many people in the nuclear age constitute a replacement of belief in the ultimacy of Divinity by belief in the efficacy of nuclear power. He sees this heretical vision as composed of four characteristics: "power viewed narrowly as 'violence,' life together in the world seen in terms of 'zero-sum gaming,' future hope deformed into 'worst case analysis,' and faith misconstrued as 'official optimism.' " Power equals violence when all human relationships are seen as conflict in which there are always winners and losers. Chapman notes that a large segment of society has adopted Thomas Hobbes' grim view of human behavior as "that condition which is called war; and such a war as is of every man against every man." Metaphors of conflict drawn from sports and war describe much of our human interaction. Some researchers believe the make-believe violence that bombards us on television and in the movies causes people to feel that the real world is even more violent than it actually may be. Second, zero-sum gaming views human resources as fixed or even declining. This means that what one person gains another must lose. Third, worst-case analysis exaggerates the strength of the enemy and underestimates our own strength. Although in actual combat this may be a successful strategy, the practice often substitutes for reality and is acted on as though it were real, as in the response of U.S. defense spending to inflated estimates of Soviet nuclear capability. This distortion encourages people to view themselves as having no control over events, helpless to do anything. Finally, official optimism is a superficial acceptance of images of reality, both positive and negative, that distort the complexities of an issue, a person or a nation. These images are conveyed by the photo ops and the thirty seconds of prose of the TV commercial. Chapman describes the "quite different perspectives on the ultimacy and wholeness of reality...offered by the world's great religions...[in Christianity] one can find an alternate vision: paradigms of power as relational and nonviolent; life together as expansive love upheld by the Spirit's fullness; the future as a shared fulfillment...in trust that God is in all and through all."[12]

Related to the view of nuclearism as heresy is the question of the ethics of deterrence. Are we willing to launch a first-strike nuclear attack? What provocation would trigger that decision? Or would we be willing to launch a retaliatory strike? If the answer to these questions is yes, then we would be complicitous in creating destruction of unimaginable magnitude. Is it imaginable that we would be willing to destroy the world in order to save it? If the answer is no, we must question the ethics of threatening to do something we have no intention of doing without any control over the effect of our bluff on the enemy—a poker game for ultimate stakes.[13]

As important as they are for theology and our resulting behavior, these two issues—ecology and nuclearism—are not the only critical challenges that human beings face in the contemporary world. Widespread poverty, political oppression, and ignorance on a global scale take more lives and destroy more human potential than do war and environmental degradation. The presence of domestic violence, which oppresses women and children at all levels of every society also adds to the experiences out of which we find the raw materials for our theological understandings and our actions. The faithful Christian cannot live in this world and pretend that these challenges do not exist; nor can he or she fail to work toward solutions with creativity, compassion, and hope.

Official Christendom has responded with unprecedented leadership to the challenges of our time. Using denominational authority to call the attention of its members to the problems of the contemporary world and offering a wide range of motivating strategies, many denominations are focusing on the obligation of Christian discipleship in the post-modern world. A brief review of the efforts of a few major Christian denominations provides a context for the development of a concept of the pursuit of peace in the RLDS Church.

In 1963 Pope John XXIII released an encyclical entitled *Pacem in Teris* (Peace on Earth). Because of the immense authority of the Pope for millions of people in Western culture, this document was an important event in the history of religious and political thought. It upheld up principles of justice and the dignity of each person. Founded on those basic principles, the document insists, are the protection of human rights and the obligations of each person in relationships. Appealing to all people of goodwill, the Pope wrote: "...the fundamental principle on which...peace depends must be replaced by another, which declares that the true and solid peace of nations consists not in equality of arms but in mutual trust alone." Although acknowledging the groundbreaking nature of the document, critics have noted that the appeal should include all people, not just those of goodwill. They also comment on the Pope's failure to answer the difficult question of when coercion is a just expression of power and when it is not.[14]

In 1983 the National Conference of Catholic Bishops authored "The Challenge of Peace: God's Promise and Our Response, A Pastoral Letter on War and Peace." The letter addressed the problems of war, military service, and the use of nuclear weapons. The bishops declared that, for Christians, some principles are morally binding while others allow for diversity of opinion. Recognizing just-war principles, the bishops reminded the reader that the arms race is not an end in itself, neither does it provide the security it promises. It also is seen as an act of aggression against the poor, depriving them of the economic resources that are used instead for armament. The document calls for disarmament based on treaties and inspection, and recognizes an increasingly interdependent political and economic world. It affirms the human dignity of every individual and calls on faithful disciples to promote human rights. Finally it proclaims:

> Peacemaking is not an optional commitment. It is a requirement of our faith. We are called to be peacemakers, not by some movement of the moment but by our Lord Jesus. The content and context of our peacemaking is set not by some political agenda or ideological program, but by the teaching of his Church.[15]

Protestant churches in the United States have been outspoken in challenging their members to adopt an active peacemaking vocation. In 1986 the United Methodist Council of Bishops issued "In Defense of Creation: The Nuclear Crisis and a Just Peace." Its stated purpose was to encourage and equip members to become knowledgeable witnesses to the power of God in Christ to bring peace to the human family. "We hope that the United Methodist people will overcome their 'nuclear numbness,' find their voices and speak and act for nuclear disarmament." The bishops condemned any nuclear action as a futile effort that would have disastrous consequences for all of creation. Members were challenged to empower themselves as peacemakers through study of other cultures, of conflict resolution skills, of the causes of war. Methodists were urged to envision alternative futures for the world. Calling itself a "just peace church," the United Church of Christ acknowledged that because war no longer means what it used to mean, the concepts of just war and crusade no longer apply. Citing the nature of modern conflict, the transference of wealth from poorer to richer countries, oppressive political systems, civil strife, and apocalyptic despair, the church called on its members to respond in creative ways to the new challenges.[16] The United Presbyterian Church in "The Believers' Calling" deplored the wasteful global expenditures for armaments. The document builds a rationale to identify peacemaking as the center of the church's mission in the modern world. In response to this objective, a number of fine educational resources have been developed to assist members in understanding and implementing this mission.

Several churches, in an attempt to help their membership own the concepts of peace and justice, engaged in extensive dialogues before issuing statements. For example, in 1983 the Dutch Roman Catholic bishops published a "Pastoral Letter on Peace and Justice." Before it was written, the bishops sponsored a "discussion round" at the parish level in which 40,000 people participated. More than 2,200 written comments also became part of the process. The Netherlands Reformed Church asked 1,500 congregations to comment on a draft of its "Pastoral Letter on Atomic Weapons" and received more than 700 responses, which were considered before the final document was finished. The United Methodist bishops' pastoral letter was also the result of a long process of consultation.[17]

Several Christian churches in the United States have, in recent years, supported their young people in choosing conscientious objection as an alternative to military service. A good example is the effort of the Episcopal Church, which has promulgated resources and procedures to help the young person conform to legal requirements to establish a conscientious objector status. Official statements on war and peace entitled "Cross Before Flag" and "To Make Peace" offer guidance from the Christian tradition to individuals faced with the conflicting demands of church and country.

A general reading of all these documents reveals many similarities between denominations in their attitude toward war and peace. The statements agree on four major points: peace in this world is a central theme of the Christian message; war is sinful and represents human failure; Christians are called to work for peace; human dignity, freedom, and the economic means to achieve potential are God's will for all human beings.

None of the positions and documents described are pacifist in the long-standing tradition of the three traditional peace churches—the Mennonites, Quakers, and the United Brethren. The influence exerted by these churches on the larger society has been far beyond their small numbers. Best known is the work of the American

Friends Service Committee whose work for peace and social justice earned the group a Nobel Peace Prize in 1947. Descended from European origins in the Waldensians, the Hutterites, and Swiss Brethren, they were separatist by tradition. In the United States they entered the political arena during World War I by becoming involved in developing provisions for conscientious objection. Meeting in 1935 Quakers, Mennonites, and Brethren adopted eight "Principles of Christian Peace and Patriotism," a major statement of the traditional Christian sectarian opposition to war and violence, but at the same time linking that tradition to internationalism:

> As members of the Historic Peace Churches we love our country and sincerely work for its highest welfare. True love for our country does not mean a hatred of others. It is our conviction that only the application of the principles of peace, love, justice, liberty, and international goodwill will make for the highest welfare of our country; and the highest welfare of our country must harmonize with the highest welfare of humanity everywhere....We feel that we are true patriots because we build upon the eternal principles of right which are the only foundations of stable government in our world community.[18]

In February 1993 the Mennonite Central Committee adopted a new statement of principle. It consists of ten sections as follow in abridged form: (1) a desire to share the good news that the grace of God is available to all people; (2) the church is a community of love to be shared with every human being; (3) Christian vocation calls believers to relieve human need and suffering; (4) relationships of love and mutual respect are worthy goals; (5) believers are called to pray for and witness to civil authorities on matters of war, relief of human need, and environmental practices; (6) believers will show by their lives that war is an unacceptable way to solve human conflict; (7) evil and oppression will be resisted in the nonviolent spirit of Jesus; (8) believers will work to discern what God's reign means for individual lifestyles and economic systems; (9) efforts will be made to find ways to protect God's creation; and (10) God's peace comes through the study of scripture, the giving and receiving of counsel, and the practice of prayer.

The Christian world, however, does not speak with one voice. In 1991 Pat Robertson, founder of the Christian Coalition, wrote that there is a global conspiracy by the devil to destroy America and its Christian values. Fearing the triumph of "the New Age religion of humanity," Robertson sees the fall of Communism, the press for disarmament, and the Persian Gulf War as all part of an ancient, carefully orchestrated plot to overthrow democracy and Christianity. Quoting Jeremiah, "The heart of man is deceitful above all things, and desperately wicked; who can know it?" he views human beings as inherently sinful and therefore unable to achieve a better world. He and his followers do not celebrate the growing emphasis on peace and nonviolent conflict resolution that is coming from so many quarters. He equates these efforts with three "New Age" themes: subversion and denial of divine revelation, the deification of the individual self, and (somewhat contradictorily) the submergence of the self in a global community.[19]

What of our own faith tradition? Until recently the pursuit of peace has not been an explicit emphasis in the RLDS Church. As an articulated objective, it represents a major change from our past which focused primarily on internal concerns and included high levels of conflict with, in some cases, tragic outcomes. So significant is this new emphasis that it is undoubtedly a major paradigm shift for the church.

William Juhnke has discovered significant ambiguity regarding peace and violence in our tradition. The Book of Mormon depicts attitudes and actions that run the gamet from pacifism to divinely sanctioned executions and aggressive war. The story of Enoch in the Inspired Version describes a peaceable kingdom where justice and peace and economic equality prevailed. The 200-year golden age of peace in the Book of Mormon was the response of the people to the ministry of Christ. In contrast, however, the behavior of early church members was more typical of the violent behavior of frontier America. Joseph Smith, sounding at times like an Old Testament prophet, called for vengeance upon his enemies "unto the third and fourth generation." Whether or not the Danite organization was his idea, it came into being during his lifetime. Even though the rhetoric of some early preachers may have been metaphoric, Missourians, with some justification, believed that the church intended to replace the U.S. government with its own theocracy, by force if necessary. In 1838 the looting and burning of Gallatin, Missouri, by church vigilantes, exceeded self-defense. At Nauvoo belligerence toward the surrounding gentile community characterized the rhetoric and actions of the Nauvoo Legion with Joseph Smith as its general. Violence also marked the reaction of church leaders to what was perceived as disloyalty in the ranks of the church.[20]

Peace was lifted up in the early Reorganization in the choice of the church seal. Adopted in 1874, the lion, lamb, and child symbolize the peace of all creation. Leaders of the Reorganization struggled with the dilemma of their own participation in armed conflict and attempted to define what the church's attitude should be toward war and peace. Deeply committed to the Northern cause in the Civil War, Joseph Smith III made an agonized decision not to enlist because of his ministerial function but said, if called, he would serve. In 1861, Joseph Smith III gave an impassioned and public endorsement of the Civil War and urged young men to volunteer for military service. Addressing the church as the new editor-in-chief of the *Herald*, he reminded his readers that

> ...the Saints should not fight their own battles for the redress of their wrongs, or for revenge upon those who injure them....However,...when the law of this land makes it the imperative duty of any of the Saints to take up arms, with no provision for an escape, then we are not at liberty to disregard the law of the land, but if there be a provision for an escape without violation of law, then they who have so learned the law of the church must justifiably avail themselves of that provision.[21]

Gary Logan has identified three *Herald* articles by church presidents in the twentieth century that articulate the church's position on peace, war, and military service. Writing in the November 18, 1939, *Herald*, President Frederick M. Smith reminded the church of its traditional support for peace.

> We are bound to stand for peace, to lift up the ensign of peace; to maintain peace in our own midst as well as with neighbors. Our motto is peace; and the whole work of the church as a religious organization centers about the development and maintenance of brotherly love or fraternity, which is the essence of peace when it becomes dynamic.

Addressing the question of military service, he cited Section 112 of the Doctrine and Covenants, which states that God has established government for the benefit of human beings. Because people benefit from the existence of government, they are duty-bound to obey its laws and mandates as long as it protects the right of individuals to hold and practice their own religious beliefs. If called to military service by the government, the individual is obligated to respond. The blood of those killed in war will be the responsibility of the governments who participate and not of the individual soldier. If a person enlists, however, the responsibility for loss of life for which he or she was directly responsible would be theirs personally. Those who have "deep scruples against bloodshed under any condition" should request some supportive service that does not require participation in direct combat. Even though President Smith believed that wars would continue until the battle of Armageddon brought down the final curtain on human history, he urged the Saints to pray for peace, work for peace, oppose war, and practice brotherly love. He understood the close relationship between the absence of war and economic justice: "[To achieve Zion] will mean not only cessation of military war but cessation of the devastating wars of commerce, industry, economics and social struggles."[22]

In a radio address delivered on January 4, 1942, President F.M. Smith appealed to all people, especially the diplomats who would design the treaties that would bring the hostilities to a close, to honor the scripture that says "God...hath made of one blood all nations of men." Undoubtedly influenced by the four freedoms identified in the Atlantic Charter, he urged respect for the needs of the defeated nations. He listed "the right of adequate space in which to live, and the use of those materials necessary to national solidarity functioning in the realm of economics, industry and trade." He called on all affluent nations, in the interests of world peace, to share their abundance with those nations whose resources were inadequate. He criticized the Christian churches for their failure to apply the principles of brotherhood to social conditions, both locally and globally. He recommended the doctrine of stewardship as the principle by which surpluses possessed by some could be shared with those in need. He believed that this religious approach to peace was the only sound basis on which lasting peace could be built.[23]

Against the background of the Korean Conflict, President Israel A. Smith again raised the problem of military service for church members. Smith quoted the entirety of the 1939 editorial by F.M. Smith and the 1865 editorial by Joseph Smith III. He expressed complete agreement with his predecessors except in the matter of volunteering for combat. He believed that loyalty to country exonerated the volunteer from responsibility for blood shed in combat sanctioned by the nation. He cited his own action in volunteering for the Spanish-American War. (He was not accepted because of poor vision.)[24]

Although the topic of peace was not a popular one for other church authors except in time of war, the *Herald* occasionally offered an article on the subject of peace. An example is the November 1935 essay by Garland Tickemyer entitled "End War Now, or Perish?" It described the uselessness of war in settling differences and reminded readers that those who rule the world by the sword would certainly perish by it. The essay did not, however, appeal to any particular RLDS tradition for support.[25] In the 1940s Deam Ferris, Evan Fry, and Elbert A. Smith discussed the issue of participation in war. In the 1960s John Bradley, Carl Mesle, Bill Russell,

Del Corey, and Wilford Winholz presented thoughtful analyses that offered a variety of viewpoints to the church's youth.

Contemporary developments can account only in part for the new emphasis on the pursuit of peace within the church. The exposure of the movement to international influences through missionary activity abroad has expanded our international outlook. Formal theological training acquired by leaders and members has acquainted us with the ideas and work of other religious groups. Clearly the most important influence, however, has been the power and authority of prophetic leadership that points to a role for the church as an "ensign of peace." The Temple bears witness to that leadership and to that intention for mission.

Virginia Bruch has identified and analyzed significant peace and justice legislative actions of the Conference since the end of World War II. These actions mark a growing concern for issues of war, peace, and social justice on the part of the church. Diffident and cautious at first, as though delegates were not sure these issues were proper subjects for action by religious groups, the consensus became stronger as delegates became more comfortable giving attention to issues outside the institution. A broad definition of peace emerges from the subject matter of these legislative actions. Resolutions in 1947 and 1986 expressed general humanitarian concern for Native Americans. At seven Conferences since 1948, legislation addressed issues of racial integration and equality and affirmed human diversity. Family issues, including reconciliation, single parents and adults, domestic violence, and aging, are present in legislation from four Conferences. Lifestyle issues address addiction and AIDS. Concern for the developmentally disabled is expressed.

At the 1960 Conference legislation directly addressed the subject of peace and justice for the first time. Although recommending cooperation with political authority, delegates voted to condemn war and supported conscientious objection as a legitimate alternative to military service. WCR 1019 was subsequently replaced by an even stronger statement (WCR 1170). Several other resolutions condemned war and offered counseling as a legal alternative to military service. A number of these were subsequently replaced by later Conferences with stronger statements as well. In 1982, WCR 1177 called on members to work for peace. The most detailed and important piece of legislation to date, this resolution deplored the use of military force and related the causes of war to injustice and inequality. Noting that at times military force is the only alternative, the statement still identifies war as sinful. Members are called on to respond to international crises with a vision beyond the limited context of national interest. The resolution called members to love and pray for all, to hope for healing and conciliation of differences, and to witness these virtues in their own behavior. This resolution also urged governmental officials to reduce and eventually eliminate nuclear armaments.

In 1964, WCR 1045 spoke to social, economic and moral problems. In 1978, WCR 1148 deplored world hunger, and in 1980, WCR 1161 affirmed the importance of human freedom and condemned injustice. In 1990, WCR 1216 directed that creative initiatives for peace and justice be included in Temple ministries.[26]

Other recent developments in the life of the church are evidence of the developing social consciousness of the institution. World Church committees on peace, human diversity, ecology, and developmental disability established by World Conference action consider both proclamation and action appropriate to the institution and to individual members. Humanitarian organizations established by church leaders and funded in large part by church members offer significant temporal and spiritual ministry throughout the world. Outreach International, established in 1979, pursues its mission to "give appropriate attention to the needs of the poor and disadvantaged consistent with the gospel of Christ and the social, economic, and educational philosophies of the church." It attempts to strengthen the problem-solving capacities of economically deprived people and provide resources that will give enabling support to the development of communities that can then sustain the realization of human potential. World Accord (Canada), Outreach Europe, and Outreach International for Community Development in Australia have all found appropriate adaptations of the original Outreach concept. In recent years the Oblation Fund has participated in worldwide efforts to alleviate human suffering.

Several major peace conferences have been convened under the auspices of the church. The first gathering took place at Kirtland in 1986 under the direction of E. J. and Charlene Gleazer who have worked tirelessly for peace since their retirement. "Becoming Makers of Peace" brought together national leaders of the peace movement as well as a significant number of church leaders. Other peace conferences have been held since.

Graceland and Park Colleges both have educational curricula in peace, and Temple School offers a number of courses. Graceland and Temple School have joined forces to offer an undergraduate program for college credit at the Temple beginning in January 1994.

Section 156, presented to the church in 1984, designated the Temple as an ensign of peace. This event has focused the attention and intention of the Reorganized Church. We have not been the first church to do so. Neither do we take a monolithic position in defining for the entire membership what peace is and what its pursuit entails. We can celebrate the response of other Christian faiths to the inspiration of God's Spirit. At the same time we can celebrate our ongoing discovery of the ways our understanding of the gospel animates our actions. Finally, each man, woman, and child who hears the call to become a peacemaker must take responsibility for developing ways appropriate to our individual pursuit of peace.

May our insights be quickened to discover in the places where we dwell the opportunities to pursue peace in response to that good Spirit that always teaches peace and that always moves ahead of us.

## Notes


1. Ulrich Mauser, *The Gospel of Peace: A Scriptural Message for Today's World* (Louisville, Kentucky: Westminister/John Knox Press, 1989).
2. James E. Will, *A Christology of Peace* (Louisville, Kentucky: Westminster/John Knox Press, 1989), 110.
3. Ibid., 141.
4. Quoted in Carl Sagan, "To Avert A Common Danger," *Parade* (March 1, 1992): 12–14.
5. Ibid.
6. Quoted in Sallie McFague, *Models of God: Theology for an Ecological, Nuclear Age* (Phildelphia: Fortress Press, 1987), 9.
7. *A Global Perspective: The Economy and the Environment*, Ellen Hoffman, ed. (American Council on Education; May 1993), 1.
8. Gordon D. Kaufman, *Theology for a Nuclear Age* (Manchester, England: The Westminster Press, 1985).

9. Jonathan Schell, *The Fate of the Earth* (New York: Avon Books, 1982), 117.
10. Henry Nelson Wieman, *The Source of Human Good* (Chicago: University of Chicago Press, 1946), 37.
11. William Hand, "The Road Ahead In the Light of the H-Bomb," *Readers' Digest,* (August 1954): 8.
12. G. Clarke Chapman, "Approaching Nuclearism as a Heresy," in Ira Chernus and Edward Linenthal, eds., *A Shuddering Dawn: Religious Studies and the Nuclear Age* (Albany, New York: State University of New York Press, 1989), 125–139.
13. Ibid.
14. Paul Tillich, *Theology of Peace*, ed. Ronald H. Stone (Louisville, Kentucky: Westminster/John Knox Press, 1990), 174–178.
15. National Conference of Catholic Bishops, "The Challenge of Peace: God's Promise and Our Response," A Pastoral Letter on War and Peace (May 3, 1983).
16. Peace Theology Development Team, *A Just Peace Church* (New York: United Church Press, 1986), 15–33.
17. James E. Will, *A Christology of Peace* (Louisville, Kentucky: Westminster/John Knox Press, 1989), 135.
18. Donald F. Durnbaugh, ed., *On Earth Peace* (Elgin, Illinois: The Brethren Press, 1978), 31–32.
19. Pat Robertson, *The New World Order* (Dallas, Texas: Word Publishing, 1991), 174.
20. William E. Juhnke, unpublished paper presented at the Mormon History Association (May 1993); Stephen C. LeSueur, *The 1838 Mormon War in Missouri* (Columbia, Missouri: University of Missouri Press, 1990); author's unpublished dissertation, "Preaching in the Latter Day Saint Church: 1830–1846," University of Missouri (1961), 146–147.
21. Ronald E. Romig and John H. Siebert, "Contours of the Kingdom: An RLDS Perspective on the Legions of Zion," *Restoration Studies V*, Darlene Caswell, ed. (Independence, Missouri: Herald Publishing House, 1993), 25–40.
22. F.M. Smith, "Our Attitude in War," *Saints' Herald* (November 18, 1939): 1443–1445.
23. F.M. Smith, "The Church and Peace," *Saints' Herald* (March 21, 1942): 359–361.
24. I.A. Smith, "Our Attitude on Military Service, *Saints' Herald* (January 1951): 12–14.
25. Garland E. Tickemyer, "End War Now, or Perish!" *Saints' Herald* (November 5, 1935): pp. 1417–1418.
26. Virginia Bruch, "The Nature of the R.L.D.S. Church's Commitment to World Peace Since World War II" (n.p.: December 1992).

## Lecture Three

# Let It Begin with Me

For a very long time now many of us have been sitting around campfires singing "Let there be peace on earth, and let it begin with me." Do we really believe that, or is it just a nice sentiment intended to give us a little shiver of good feeling? Let's test our peacemaking IQ by engaging in a little personal inventory-taking. I am going to propose three categories for our inventory process. First, what are our assumptions about peacemaking? Second, what do we understand about the peacemaking process (remembering that "There is no way to peace; peace is the way.")? Third, what do we identify as the peacemaking skills in those especially blessed people whom we have seen making peace?

***1. What are our assumptions about peace? Do we believe peace is possible and is a worthy goal?*** Peace exists on all levels of our experience—interpersonal, community, national and international. Peacemaking is dynamic, not static. Peace does not exclude conflict but implies a willingness and a competence to approach conflict nonviolently and creatively. Conflict can have positive outcomes to the benefit of everyone involved. Peace requires us to change, both internally and externally—avoiding violence and working creatively to discover new solutions to old problems. Peace takes constant attention and is very hard work; it requires patience. Yitzhak Rabin spoke for all of us when he said: "It is not easy."

***2. What do we understand about the peacemaking process?*** It is action oriented, even proactive. Peacemaking requires specific skills that can be learned through experience, study, and research. Peacemaking may intervene at different stages of conflict. Peacemaking recognizes differences and often clarifies them. It is not, as generations of mothers have thought, the "smoothing over" of differences, which usually leaves them intact to rear their heads again in different guise another day. Peacemaking can create justice in both micro and macro human communities and can facilitate the growth of human rights and values.

***3. What are some peacemaking skills?*** First among these would be internal attitudes, insights, and feelings; sensitivity to the feelings of others; and resources of character and spirit, including sincerity and integrity. External skills include communication ability, analysis, imaging, strategizing, educating, and training. As we acknowledge that peace is possible, we will be motivated to explore the world of peacemaking possibilities for the individual, and the nature of many of these skills will become clearer.

The following examples are real, and they illustrate the power and the possibilities of the peacemaking process between individuals and groups in many situations in our society:

Delbert Ranney, high priest and Marine lieutenant-colonel, received orders to command the squadron of attack aircraft in Vietnam. When he arrived to take up his assignment, he found the squadron in disarray. Performance was poor and the men's morale was very low. During his years in the Marines, Del had observed that hard-nosed, tough, mean leadership if combined with fairness usually appeared to be effective. However, he did not find in that style the respect, caring, and love that he valued. He decided to try another approach. He first called together the senior noncommissioned officers and challenged them to help him create a unit that cared and protected each member, showed concern for the men's problems back home, and that tried to heal the place and people who were their neighbors. He wandered around day and night listening to the men, getting to know them personally, and asking about their work and their families. When discipline or reprimand were needed, he responded appropriately but did not humiliate the person. He would not tolerate viciousness. One flyer habitually expressed his pleasure in killing and talked about the Vietnamese as though they were subhuman. Del used his authority to stop that kind of talk. One member of the ground crew, either from conscience, fear, or both, could not bring himself to load bombs. Del reassigned him. The unit morale gradually improved. The men organized and supported an orphanage in a nearby village. They protected and cared for each other off duty. Carelessness and sabotage by the ground crews disappeared. The unit record received a commendation from Washington. The men's regard for Del was overwhelming. As the men rotated home, they called his wife, Cathy, to express their appreciation to her for the way Del's leadership had helped them feel good about themselves. In the midst of war Del Ranney had made peace.

In 1975, the American Friends Service Committee received a request from some Vietnamese citizens to provide badly needed hospital equipment, screw making machines, and fish nets. The U.S. Department of the Treasury, acting on specific instructions from President Gerald Ford, refused to issue the export licenses. The committee decided to "follow conscience" and go forward with the shipments. They knew that the consequences of their action could be fines and imprisonment. Organizers informed Congress and the media of the situation and of their intention to move ahead. Demonstrations in support of the project took place in some forty cities across the country. Individuals contributed money and signed a statement acknowledging their voluntary participation in the project. In a short time the government issued the licenses. Confrontation but not violence ended in success.

During the early days of busing in a small Tennessee town, black students found themselves being treated disrespectfully by white bus drivers. For example, the driver would stop in front of the homes of white students, but black students were allowed off only at the regular stops. Drivers were verbally abusive to the black students who decided to retaliate by beating up some of the bus drivers. One black mother learned of the plan and spread the word. For the next few days black mothers and grandmothers rode the buses. When the school superintendent learned what was going on, he informed the drivers he would not tolerate abusive or discriminatory behavior, and he and school board members rode the buses themselves to monitor the situation. Proaction prevented violence and the unjust treatment ceased.

A student teacher wanted a more active, creative role in the classroom, but the regular teacher was reluctant to allow her more freedom. Anger and avoidance became the pattern of their interaction until the supervising professor called a meeting and facilitated a discussion of the perceptions and feelings of each. They explored possible solutions, and creative ideas emerged from the discussion. The children in the classroom benefited from the new relationship. The skillful intervention of the college professor resolved a conflict that had the potential of spoiling an important developmental experience.

Terje Roed Larsen, a Norwegian social science professor, taking advantage of his scholarly network in the Middle East, brought together high-ranking representatives of the PLO and Israel for secret talks which led to the Recognition Agreement signed in Washington in September 1993. An invitation to talk, a series of meetings, and skillful mediation broke a deadlock that had existed so long it had become a habit.

Thus the peacemaking process is powerful when people of vision and skill, high principle and goodwill set out to achieve a worthy goal, even in an environment of extreme hostility.

Peacemaking skills have become the focus of the relatively new field of conflict resolution, a process that has the potential to become one of the most effective techniques for large numbers of people to learn how to make peace. In the past, the methods of choice for dealing with conflict have been confrontation and even violence, articulated in the win/lose language of sports and war.

Our current litigiousness is not new. From our earliest history as a nation observers like Alexis de Tocqueville have commented on the speed with which we make use of the judicial system to ajudicate disagreements.[1] Notwithstanding the demonstrated strengths and benefits of our legal system, this recourse to legal process usurps the power of the individual over his or her own disputes. Courts and governmental agencies have acquired many of the same disadvantages: long waits, expensive representation, red tape, and adversarial procedures. So often the emphasis on right and wrong, on winner and loser, destroys the relationship between the people involved. The mediating of disputes between individuals or small groups which once was done by the extended family, the church, or by leading citizens of the community is no longer easily available in our highly mobile and predominately urban society. Law professor and former Harvard president, Derek Bok, has noted that our legal system is "strewn with the disappointed hopes of those who find [it] too complicated to understand, too quixotic to command respect, and too expensive to be of much practical use."[2] Laurence Tribe, his colleague in the Harvard Law School, agrees that the system is characterized by "too much law, too little justice; too many rules, too few results...."[3]

Contemporary society is finding many roles for the techniques of extra-legal conflict resolution. It is beginning to supplement or replace many of the traditional disciplinary practices of schools, courtroom litigation, and adversarial legislative processes. From dysfunctional family disputes to global crises, these methods are gaining increasing respect and use. Developed almost exclusively by the private sector and varying widely in technique, this new approach to dealing with conflict tries to find alternatives to doing nothing or escalating conflict. The process is informal and private and allows the people involved to be active participants in working toward a solution. Its recent origins are found in governmental conciliation and mediation services, which have existed since the early 1930s. In the mid-1970s, utilizing the experience of these earlier efforts, a network of neighborhood justice centers where community volunteers help people settle their own disputes came into existence. Concerned with the deteriorating reputation of the legal profession, Chief Justice Warren E. Burger convened a Conference on the Causes of Popular Dissatisfaction with the Administration of Justice in 1976. This conference recommended to the legal establishment alternative ways to settle disputes. The result was a proliferation of processes and techniques that have proved efficacious.[4]

Responding to these fresh ideas about conflict resolution, individuals in positions of authority are investigating how their specific challenges can be met in new ways. Corporate executives and government officials are seeking training to learn how to deal with employees, customers, constituents, and competition. For example, the Iowa Mediation Service came into being during the farm crisis of the early 1980s to help farmers and creditors find alternatives to bankruptcy and foreclosure. Achieving a highly successful record, the service has expanded its efforts to include a Victim Offender Reconciliation Program and is beginning, in conjunction with the Iowa Peace Institute, to address the problem of gang violence in Iowa. It also offers workshops to train mediators.[5] Dispute settlement firms have been created to provide mediation services, and the ombudsperson has become a standard box on the organizational chart.

Families are also turning to mediation to help their members manage conflicts. Several hundred local dispute settlement firms have sprung up across the country. Governmental agencies—for example, the Equal

Employment Opportunity Commission—require complainants to attempt to settle disputes using conflict resolution agencies before going to court. Law professors are beginning to teach dispute settlement, and practicing attorneys are studying new ways of settling cases.

Elementary and secondary schools across the country are training their own students to act as conflict managers. One public school in a California inner city reports a reduction in violence of 70 percent as a direct and dramatic result of peer conflict management efforts. Students proudly wear T-shirts identifying them as conflict managers. When a dispute occurs on the playground or in the school building, the student moves in and offers the disputants two alternatives: cooperate with peer mediation or go to the principal (peer mediation is usually the choice.) Many public agencies are following a process of negotiated rulemaking in which interested parties can negotiate new regulations. Finally, there was the magnificent achievement at Camp David in 1978 where, during thirteen arduous days, President Jimmy Carter mediated an agreement between Anwar Sadat and Menachem Begin, representing Egypt and Israel.

The benefits of this process are clear: settlements are achieved sooner than if they were litigated; the process is less costly; individuals feel they have control over their own affairs; continuing relationships between the disputants are more likely to be preserved. Furthermore, a growing body of evidence suggests that settlements reached by this process are more likely to be honored by those involved because the participants helped develop them and take ownership of them. At the same time negotiated settlements have some shortcomings. They do not develop precedent, and they have no power to punish wrongdoers. However, although not a perfect system, the alternative dispute resolution (ADA) movement has made an important place for itself in contemporary society, a place that has provided some badly needed new ways of doing business. This development is undoubtedly part of a new social phenomenon that has found expression in many areas of life. New ways of looking at relationships have called into question the absolute and authoritarian practices of the past. Acknowledging the increasing complexity of issues and questioning the efficacy of the adversarial habits of the past, individuals are insisting on collaborative problem solving in which power is shared and consensus is sought. Included in the process is everyone who can contribute a point of view and who has power to make, implement, take responsibility for, or block solutions. The goal is for a group to come to a decision that participants can live with and support. The process is not finished until the participants express willingness to sell the solution to a larger group.

Although a wide variety of techniques exist, the problem-solving process usually identifies six goals: (1) to define the problem; (2) to identify all possible options; (3) to clarify any that may be ambiguous and to evaluate all options; (4) to decide on the most acceptable one; (5) to develop a plan for implementation; and (6) to develop a process for evaluation.

The mediator plays an important role in the process of resolving or managing conflict. The process is structured in a similar way, whether the conflict manager is a fifth-grade elementary school student or an employee of the U.S. Mediation and Conciliation Service. When the group gathers, the mediator makes an opening statement that describes how the session will be conducted. He or she emphasizes the confidentiality of the occasion and compliments and encourages the disputants. The mediator explains the rules of the session: no name calling, no interrupting, no abusive language. The second step provides uninterrupted time for each person to explain what is happening and how he or she feels about it. The exchange segment has been compared, from the perspective of the mediator, to a rodeo rider outlasting a bucking horse. The disputants respond to issues, accusations, and questions. This process allows information to be gathered and feelings to be vented. The fourth step is the building of the agreement. The mediator and the disputants can now identify and describe the few really important issues that have risen to the top. The mediator stops frequently to be sure everyone involved is in agreement with this identification and description. The final step is the crafting of an agreement in writing. It is detailed as to who is to do what and when. Procedures for handling future problems are included. The agreement is signed by the disputants. The mediator closes the session with an encouraging and complimentary statement.

This method of dispute settlement assumes that people are willing and able to change their behavior, and that they want to be responsible for it. It also assumes that disputants prefer friendly, honest, open, and cooperative solutions and that they appreciate being respected as experts on their own problems. When people have worked hard to craft solutions to disputes, they are more likely to live up to the agreement. The entire process is a "reality check" for the people involved, helping them see beyond the rationalizations and painful emotions that cloud their perception of the issues. The process helps people redirect their energies away from aggrieved feelings and take control of their own behavior. It facilitates the discovery of creative new ideas to govern relationships.[6]

Another method finding favor with some mediators and particularly useful for those responsible for a deliberative process (such as committee chairs, presiding officers, and pastors) is the "colored hat" technique used to assign thinking tasks to members of the deliberating group. This method departs somewhat from argument and dialectic, habits deeply ingrained in Western rational thinking. The system is based on the assumption that argument and dialectic do not necessarily stimulate the generative and creative energies that are often most effective. Each individual in the deliberative group assumes responsibility for one way of "looking at the elephant." The hat metaphor makes explicit a variety of perspectives. The white hat is the computer, neutral and objective: "Just the facts please." The red hat contributes the emotional perspective. The black hat is the "It can't be done for the following reasons" person. The yellow hat is optimistic, believing that a good solution will be found. The green hat is a brainstormer, creative and generative. Finally the blue hat facilitates the contributions of the other hats, ensuring fairness and organizing the contributions of each hat. If all members of the group understand their roles, the group process can be as explicit as the following comment: "When you say that you are wearing your red hat"; or, "Now I am going to put on my black hat for a moment to remind us that...". This technique, although highly artificial, is fun and causes participants to take themselves a little less seriously and develop a broader perspective on the issue.[7]

Intentional peacemaking skills are becoming much more important in the repertoire of today's leaders. We have known leaders who appear to have learned how to win by intimidation. Repression of opposition and authoritarianism have become less and less acceptable, however. As we have already seen from Del Ranney's experience, leadership responsibility presents the individual with a grand opportunity to build ethical behavior. The leader can, for example, ensure that peacemaking is an important attribute of the institutional culture. Peacemaking leadership models and encourages equality, mutuality, and recognition of the inherent worth of all persons, no matter what their role in the organization.

Management theorists have analyzed this leadership behavior: the leader takes responsibility for interpersonal relationships in the organization, assembles a team that includes a variety of styles, works to create a family environment, manages by wandering around for the primary purpose of listening carefully to what employees have to say, praises good work, pushes decision-making to the level of the people who are most affected, seeks to build consensus, and gives special attention to articulating the mission of the institution. Instead of emphasizing hierarchy and privilege, separateness and independence, this leader sees the human relationships within the organization as an interconnecting web, each part affected by other parts, and each person seeing himself or herself as a collaborator with other members of the organization. Many executives who have given up the old authoritarian modes and who have sincerely implemented these practices have been astonished and pleased with the release of energy and creativity that individuals within the organization have achieved.[8] If these leadership behaviors are important in the workplace, how much more important they are in an organization, like the congregation or the service club that depends for its life on volunteers. This view of leadership style is clearly an application of Christian principles to the workplace and the congregation.

In his book *The Seven Habits of Highly Effective People*, Stephen Covey identifies Habit 4 as "Think Win/Win." He describes six paradigms of human interaction: first, "Win/lose"; second, "lose/win"; third, "lose/lose"; fourth, "win"; fifth, "win/win"; and sixth, "win/win or no deal." Western culture, Covey believes, has emphasized the "win/lose" exchange. Competition, comparison, power, credentials, and possessions are all means of winning at someone else's expense. In "lose/win" some people give in to avoid conflict even at the expense of fairness and justice. "Lose/lose" occurs when two highly competitive people who are each in the habit of winning lock horns and lose sight of all other values except winning. No matter how the issue is finally resolved, the enormous psychic cost makes each individual a loser. People who think "win" simply ignore the presence of any other interest. Each person is for himself or herself. "Win/win" looks for mutual benefit and sees cooperation rather than competition as the best modus operandi. It affirms, "It's not your way or my way; it's a better way, a higher way." The sixth paradigm is "win/win or no deal." Believing that "win/win" is the only acceptable alternative, the participants agree that nothing will be done if "win/win" cannot be achieved. For example, Covey explains, family members who cannot agree on which video to rent will decide to do something else with their Saturday evening.

Achieving "win/win" requires character and moves toward the kind of relationship out of which agreement can emerge. Covey believes that character is composed of two elements: integrity and maturity. A person of integrity knows his or her value system and does not compromise those values, balancing a mature courage in support of principle with an empathic consideration of the feelings of others. In addition to character, Covey describes a personality characteristic that he calls "abundance mentality." A person with a scarcity mentality sees reality as having a fixed number of assets. Thus any redistribution of assets increases their number at one spot and reduces their number at another. From an inner sense of personal worth and security, an individual with an abundance mentality, on the other hand, believes in an unlimited number of assets. Paradoxically, the number always increases as the assets are used up. Covey describes relationships in terms of emotional bank accounts to which deposits are added or from which deposits are withdrawn. This accounting metaphor describes an interaction that grows out of goodwill and generosity. Finally, the agreement that results from character and relationships focuses on results, not methods. The elements of the agreement should be very clear to all participants, and after that people should be free to find their own ways to the outcome.[9]

Peace begins with us. Peace also begins with our children. Gandhi noted that "If we are to reach real peace in the world, we shall have to begin with children."[10] The most important way we can break the old patterns of violence is with the children. We can start the peace process by taking responsibility for the peaceful socialization of the next generation. For many children, peace, when compared to war, is strange and boring. The Russian writer of children's stories, Surmeil Marchak, describes a conversation with two of his grandchildren. He asked them what they were playing. They replied "We are playing at war." Marchak suggested that they should play at peace because war is bad. After some thought they replied, "Granddad, how do you play at peace?"[11]

We are appalled at the escalating levels of violence among and to our young people. The Children's Defense Fund reported in January 1994 that homicide is the third leading cause of deaths for elementary and middle-school children. The equivalent of a full classroom of children is killed by guns every two days in the United States. Since 1979 as many children and teens have been killed as American casualties in the Vietnam War. In the United States a child is fifteen times as likely to die from gunfire as a child in Northern Ireland.[12] Four years ago 22 percent of teens surveyed said they felt unsafe in school. This year the figure has jumped to 37 percent.[13] No region of the country is immune. For example, a dramatic increase in juvenile crime in Iowa, a state where crime statistics are low compared to national figures, has been documented.[14] In September 1993, in response to the increasingly dangerous situation in its public schools, the state of Colorado enacted legislation making it unlawful for minors to possess semiautomatic weapons. That this was a necessary action is terrible evidence of how out of control the weapon situation is in our country.

If it were not so serious, the argument that made the news during Christmas 1993 over the talking Barbie and GI Joe dolls would be funny. A group supporting nondiscrimination switched voice tapes on the talking dolls. GI Joe said, "Let's go shopping." Barbie stated, "Dead men tell no lies." The point of the switch was to dramatize the sexual discrimination perpetrated by the makers of the toys, not to protest the socializing influence of the vicious message on the one hand and the trivial one on the other.

We have clearly not done a very good job of teaching our children to be peacemakers. Admittedly a difficult task in a culture where images of violence abound, where Rambo, Dirty Harry, and the Terminator are cult heros, families and churches will have to work hard to reclaim an initiative that has been taken over by the toy industry, television, and the movies.

There is good experimental evidence to suggest that children who have been treated with respect and whose character, responsibility, and resourcefulness have been developed do not need violent behavior to give them a feeling of power and self-worth. Furthermore, a strong sense of self is necessary to develop compassion for others and the security to take public risks for good purposes. Self-esteem is built not so much from focusing on the likes and dislikes of the individual or from finding many ways to deliver the message that the child is special. These may be outcomes of self-esteem rather than the means. The means may be an increasing ability on the part of the child to experience the world with a sense of awe, to reflect, raise questions, and generate alternative solutions to practical and intellectual problems.[15] Engaging in significant activities gives even very young children a sense of importance and meaning.

In 1987 I visited several elementary classrooms in the Soviet Union. As a teacher accustomed to Western dialectical practice, I did not find much to admire there.

One exception, however, was the real work that occupied a small part of every class day. The children were separating different screws, nails, and other hardware to be delivered to a factory that made large trucks. The children were praised for their speed and commended by the factory authorities for their good work. They proudly showed me their system for doing the work. It was obviously the result of careful thought to produce a maximum of efficiency, and the children who had devised certain features of the system were identified and accepted our congratulations. Clearly the whole group found self-esteem in this activity.

One of the evidences of a growing attention to peace is the availability of many resources to assist parents in helping children learn how to participate in the process of peacemaking. Parenting for Peace and Justice, a St. Louis-based organization, has identified and created many good materials. The organization recommends children's games, literature, and family activities that uphold peacemaking values. Many games are now available that teach children techniques of peace and provide information for life in the global village. One is "Children of the World: Your Passport to Places New and Far," a game that compares the customs and daily life of children in four countries. Old games can be given new and noncompetitive twists. For example, Bingo can have as its objective a group effort to fill all the squares, or Scrabble can challenge all of the players to cooperate in achieving a high score. For older children, there are volunteer trips to forty-five countries and most of the states in the United States for work and education.

Parenting for Peace and Justice suggests many family activities: use mealtime to talk about what is in the news; place a world map in a prominent place and refer to it often and use world map placemats at the table; talk and learn about the lives of people in other cultures and cultivate friendship with refugees or international visitors; identify local and international peacemakers; create a good news bulletin board to emphasize the good things happening worldwide; discuss ethnic names and background; encourage the learning of a second language; support UNICEF; observe the holidays of other cultures. June Teenth, Cinco de Mayo, and Yom Kippur, for example, provide opportunities to learn about the days and historical events important to others.[16]

Good children's literature presents authentic information about other cultures and presents role models from many cultures that counter racial and sexual stereotypes and that narrate the resolution of conflicts in creative and nonviolent ways. A classic of this kind is a book by Laurie Dolphin entitled *Neve Shalom: Wahat al-Salam=Oasis of Peace.* It is a beautifully illustrated book telling the story of two children—one Jewish, the other Arab—who meet at a settlement and learn to live together in peace. The Children's Peace Pavilion at the Temple is developing a library of children's literature that has been graded and identified by theme. A reading list is available by writing The Peace Center, The Temple, P.O. Box 1059, Independence, MO 64051.

Adults need to anlayze their words and behavior to be sure we are setting good examples. Do we use violent metaphors when talking with other adults or with children, or do we reveal prejudice and hatred for people who are different? Parents also need to monitor the child's exposure to violent models. Watching one of our grandsons' favorite Saturday morning cartoons, "X-Men," I found myself unable to distinguish between the good guys and the bad guys given the high level of violent behavior on the part of all the characters. Apparently gone are the days (when our children were small) when it was easy to distinguish between Dudley Doright and Snively Whiplash.

All of us should insist that the public schools provide peaceful classrooms for our children. We should insist that schools develop environments for the practice of cooperative and compassionate behavior, that children be taught self-control and the skills of conflict management, and that the materials used to teach reading as well as social studies be free of stereotypes.

Deborah Prothrow-Stith has developed a violence prevention curriculum for the public schools. It has been adopted by 324 cities in forty-five states and is used in Canada, Israel, American Samoa, and England. She describes some of the program's characteristics as it has been implemented in the Little Rock, Arkansas school system. In elementary schools there are anti-fighting campaigns with schoolwide rewards for not fighting. A peer mediation program was adopted in one elementary school with the result that there was not a single fight during the entire year. The goal in junior and senior high is to raise the consciousness of the youth by educating them about the risks of violence in general and by analyzing the violence the kids watch on TV. The program is credited with helping reduce the number of fights and suspensions within the system. Dr. Prothrow-Stith notes that grassroots efforts such as MADD (Mothers Against Drunk Driving) have been tremendously successful in achieving their goals, and she urges adults to get involved. People can make a difference.[17]

Myriam Miedzian calls our attention to the program initated at the Germantown (Pennsylvania) Friends School and adopted at nine Philadelphia public schools. This is a parenting program that educates both boys and girls in junior high about how babies develop and what impact adults have on that process. Believing that both males and females have significant potential for empathy and compassion, the program provides exposure to real babies on a continuing basis. When parents are empathetic, children are more likely to become so. When good models of parenting are held up, male students especially grow in other areas of their interpersonal relationships. Although the program is too new for any longitudinal studies to have been finished, there are some very hopeful indications that it is having a positive effect in the reduction of violent behavior among its students.[18]

In his book *Talking Peace: A Vision for the Next Generation,* former President Jimmy Carter addresses young people directly. He offers ideas for individual action. He suggests global education with special emphasis on where conflicts are occurring. He mentions support of kitchens that feed the poor, and recommends a recycling effort and neighborhood cleanup. He urges young people to join human rights organizations such as Amnesty International. He suggests starting a mediation team at school. He urges participation in local politics. He wants students to be knowledgeable about the drug and gang problems in their communities. And he recommends participation in Big Brother or Sister programs. All of these activities, he affirms, pursue peace and give the young people who participate a sense of meaning for their lives.[19]

If we really believe that peace begins with each of us, we confront a very difficult task. It is not easy to pursue peace in a culture with a long and admired history of violence. Our personal behavior must change, and we must find the courage to become agents for change within our society, a role that demands sensitivity, wisdom, and the willingness to confront those practices that do not reflect our ideals. This may well be the opportunity for the Christian to become a badly needed leaven in contemporary society. Let the beautiful promise found in Isaiah 58:9–11 (JB) inspire us:

> If you do away with the yoke, the clenched fist, the wicked word, if you give your bread to the hungry and relief to the oppressed,...[God] will always guide you, giving you relief in desert places. [God] will give strength to your bones and you shall be like a watered garden, like a spring of water whose waters never run dry.

Peace does begin with each of us—first in our hearts, then in all the places where we live and work, and in those institutions on which we have influence. The pursuit of peace involves the sharing of our inspiration and the accepting of those opportunities for peacemaking that we discover and create. Thus is the gospel of Christ proclaimed to the world.

## Notes

1. Alexis de Tocqueville, *Democracy in America*, J.P. Mayer and Max Lerner, eds. (New York: Harper & Row, 1966), 241–248.
2. Derek C. Bok, "A Flawed System of Law Practice and Training," *Journal of Legal Education*, no. 33 (1983): 530.
3. Laurence Tribe, "Too Much Law, Too Little Justice," *Atlantic Monthly* (July 1979): 25.
4. Warren E. Burger, "Isn't There a Better Way?" *ABA Journal* (March 1982): 274.
5. "Ending Disputes," *The Des Moines Register* (January 2, 1993): T-2. For additional information call 515/244-8214.
6. James Lave, "Contributions of the Emerging Field of Conflict Resolution," W. Scott Thompson and Kenneth M. Jensen, eds., *Approaches to Peace: An Intellectual Map* (United States Institute of Peace, 1991), 306; David Augsburger, *Conflict Mediation Across Cultures* (Louisville, Kentucky: Westminster/John Knox Press, 1992); John Burton, *Resolving Deep Rooted Conflict* (New York: University Press of America, 1987); Roger Fisher and William Ury, *Getting to Yes: Negotiating Agreement Without Giving In* (New York: Penguin Books, 1981); Donald Horowitz, *Ethnic Groups in Conflict* (Berkeley, California: University of California Press, 1985); Speed Leas, *Moving Your Church Through Conflict* (Washington, D.C.: Alban Institute, 1985); William Ury, Jeanne Brett, and Stephen Goldberg, *Getting Disputes Resolved* (San Francisco: Josey-Bass, 1988); Deborah Tannen, *You Just Don't Understand* (New York: Morrow, 1990).
7. Edward de Bono, *Six Thinking Hats: An Essential Approach to Business Management* (New York: Little, 1986).
8. Thomas Peters and Robert Waterman, Jr., *In Search of Excellence* (New York: Harper & Row, 1982).
9. Stephen R. Covey, *The Seven Habits of Highly Effective People* (New York: Simon & Schuster, 1989), 204–234.
10. Colman McCarthy, "Peace Education: The Time Is Now," *The Washington Post* (December 29, 1992).
11. Quoted by Leonard Sweet, *The Lion's Pride: America & the Peaceable Community* (Nashville, Tennessee: Abingdon Press, 1987), 13.
12. "Third-leading Cause of Kids' Deaths: Guns," *The Des Moines Register* (January 21, 1994): A-4.
13. "It Just Keeps Getting Worse," *USA Weekend* (August 1993): 8–13.
14. "Armed and Dangerous—A Chilling Wave of Teen Brutality," *The Des Moines Register* (September 26, 1993): A-1ff.

15. Kathleen McGinnis and Barbara Oehlberg, *Starting Out Right* (New York: Meyer-Stone Books, 1988) 306–307; Thomas Gordon, *Discipline That Works: Promoting Self-Discipline in Children at Home & at School* (New York: NAL-Dutton, 1991).
16. *Parenting for Peace & Justice Newsletter*, The Institute for Peace and Justice, Room 124, 4144 Lindell Blvd., St. Louis, MO 63108.
17. Deborah Prothrow-Stith, *Deadly Consequences: How Violence Is Destroying Our Teenage Population* (New York: Harper, 1991).
18. Myriam Miedzian, *Boys Will Be Boys: Breaking the Link Between Masculinity and Violence* (New York: Doubleday, 1991).
19. Jimmy Carter, *Talking Peace: A Vision for the Next Generation* (New York: Dutton Children's Books, 1993).

Lecture Four

# Violence and Nonviolence

Our society today verifies Hannah Arendt's view that "The practice of violence, like all action, changes the world, but the most probable change is to a more violent world."[1] The practice of violence in the United States has produced an increasing level of violence. David Gelman notes that "the culture of aggression shows up in our speech, our play and our entertainment. It's better than hip, it's commercial." He identifies a general failure of will, a kind of paralysis in the face of the growing dimensions of the problem. Our culture has become desensitized to violence by its constant repetition.[2] Is it any mystery then, that young people behave violently? They have adopted the attitudes and ethics of the adult world. The famed Navajo code talkers of World War II offer a wise warning. They not only provided unbreakable codes for the U.S. from their native language; they also participated in some of the bloodiest fighting of the war in the Pacific. But they do not talk about their experiences. Following the traditional Navajo reticence to glorify war, most of them also avoid all ceremonies and parades. They believe that talking about war contaminates the minds of impressionable young people who should not hear about bloodshed.

"There is always the danger of enticement for the young."[3]

Citizens of the United States, aided and abetted by the gun lobby, have become the most heavily armed nation on earth. Twenty-five million people in this country own 200 million guns, and the count continues to rise. The consequences are tragic. In the last twenty years firearms have been responsible for 75 percent of teenage deaths. Not only are guns immediately available but no product-safety regulations currently exist for handguns or ammunition. We cannot say that this is the way the world is. In 1990 handguns murdered ten people in Australia (another nation with a frontier history), twenty-two in Great Britain, sixty-eight in Canada, and 10,567 in the United States. We cannot blame this national problem solely on our frontier heritage or on the intention of defending ourselves from the dangers of our neighborhoods.[4]

Can we explain human violence? That question has intrigued generations of anthropologists, psychologists, and theologians. A variety of hypotheses have been offered covering a wide range of explanations and theories. Conrad Lorenz postulates a disjunction between evolutionary changes in the parts of the brain that predispose humans to violent behavior. However, he notes a strong socializing influence—society trains its members to accept and admire war and violence. Through the media and in the classroom, we teach our young that our wars are just and that the pursuit of peace is effeminate, passive, cowardly, weak, dishonorable, and even subversive. Lorenz also recognizes the power of love, acknowledging it as a gift from the Creator:

We know that, in the evolution of vertebrates, the bond of personal love and friendship was the epoch-making invention created by the real constructor when it became necessary for two or more individuals of an aggressive species to live peacefully together and to work for a common end. We know that human society is built on the foundation of this bond.[5]

Irenaus Eibl-Eibesfeldt has written, "The disposition toward intolerance and aggression is certainly innate in us, but we carry no mark of Cain upon our brows. The thesis of man's killer nature cannot be seriously upheld; on the contrary investigation shows that by nature we are also extremely friendly beings."[6] Freud described humans as driven by two contradictory forces: *eros* and *thanatos*. *Eros* is the impulse within us that strives for closer union with others and seeks to preserve and conserve. *Thanatos* is the drive or instinct that works for the dissolution of everything living or united.[7] J. Glenn Gray believes that "the satisfaction in destroying is peculiarly human, or more exactly put, devilish in a way animals can never be." He notes that violence, especially as it is acted out in war, appears to provide a meaning for human life that religion has failed to offer.[8]

The masculine mystique in our culture is responsible for much of its violence. Myriam Miedzian writes, "Many of the values of the masculine mystique, such as toughness, dominance, repression of empathy, extreme competitiveness, play a major role in criminal and domestic violence and underlie the thinking and policy decisions of many of our political leaders....The role that obsolete male modes of thought and behavior have played and continue to play in perpetuating the nuclear arms race has been recognized by an increasing number of people...." She reminds us that "while there is a growing clamor that something be done about violence in our streets and homes, there has been very little systematic analysis of what it is that reinforces violent, reckless, self-destructive behavior in boys [and men] and what can be done to change it." She believes that the generally accepted view of society, that male behavior is the norm and female behavior is deviant, makes it very difficult for men to change and very easy for women to attempt to become more like them.[9]

Another important source of violence in our society may be the impact on the young of the nuclear threat itself. Careful research on the response of children and adolescents to life in the nuclear age has revealed some startling insights into the thinking of those young people who have never known a world without the bomb. Young people revealed anger and depression and exhibited a sense of foreshortened time and a general fear of what the future holds. They thought about nuclear war with a sense of vulnerability and hopelessness. Seventh graders revealed cynicism regarding the competency of world leaders to control the international situation. The need of human beings to maintain a sense of the continuity of life in the face of personal death is frustrated by the fear that there will be no future. Robert Jay Lifton argues that "we live and allow ourselves to die by the psychic images we construct of how the self is related to the vital past, the meaningful present, and the hoped-for future." He uses the term "psychic numbness" to describe the sense of living with a doom that will extinguish the hoped-for future. Many college students, when questioned, indicated real doubt that there would be a future. Without that faith in the future, a basic human need is not met. Erik Erikson calls that need "generativity," a force concerned with establishing and guiding the next generation. When this sense is highly developed, the person's compassion extends beyond the self, the family, the tribe, even the nation. Without it, concern for anything or anyone is difficult to achieve.[10] If the atomic threat has robbed many of our youth of that hope and challenge, there is little mystery about the participation of young people in the random violence of our society. Furthermore, the effect seems to be cumulative. The disillusionment experienced by young children is shocking. A third-grader friend of mine proudly told me how much he loved mathematics and how well he was doing in that subject. Trying to affirm his achievement, I said to him, "Maybe you will grow up to be a famous mathematician." His face clouded as he replied, "I don't want to grow up to be a famous anything; I don't want to die." Searching to understand his comment, I remembered that just two weeks before, John Lennon had been gunned down in New York.

Theologian Walter Wink calls our attention to the "myth of redemptive violence" that characterized the religions of ancient Mesopotamia. He postulates that the "religion of Babylon—one of the world's oldest, continuously surviving religions—is thriving as never before in every sector of contemporary American life, even in our synagogues and churches. It, and not Christianity, is the real religion of America....this myth [of redemptive violence] undergirds American popular culture, civil religion, nationalism, and foreign policy." In the *Enuma Elish* creation story (1250 B.C.), evil existed before creation took place, and violence characterized the act of creation itself. Violence was depicted as a necessary component of the cyclical renewal of nature. Although Wink does not trace the historical continuity of this view of the universe (vis-à-vis the creation story in Genesis or the Christian ethic), he discovers in popular culture a repetition of "the simplest, laziest, most exciting, uncomplicated, irrational, and primitive depiction of evil," which indoctrinates the young into a society in which violence is a self-fulfilling prophecy. Wink cites as an example a bit of dialogue from the television sitcom "Get Smart" in which Agent 99, after witnessing the violent destruction of an enemy agent, comments, "You know, Max, sometimes I think we're no better than they are, the way we murder and kill and destroy people." Smart's response: "Why, 99, you knew we have to murder and kill and destroy in order to preserve everything that's good in the world."[11]

As we search for ways to stem the appalling increase of violence in our society. we need to think carefully about our goal. We certainly do not want to eliminate self-assertiveness and ambition among individuals or societies. Human creativity has both a destructive and a constructive face. It often challenges the status quo, and in attempting to alter it, discovers new and fresh ideas and techniques. So our goal should be to help our youth (and ourselves) achieve a dynamic equilibrium between self-assertion and respect for other people, between change and conservation.

We need to see nonviolence as a dynamic response to problems and challenges, a response that does not damage anyone emotionally or physically. Elise Boulding has found that people who work consistently to make positive changes in society share a number of characteristics, none of them negative: "They are optimistic; they are competent; they have high self-esteem; they learn easily; they are able to solve problems and resolve conflict skillfully."[12] Young people who are working to bring about a better society are less likely to exhibit Lifton's "nuclear numbness."

No discussion of violence is complete without some consideration of its ultimate form—war. War is an all-too-common fact of human history. Norman Cousins has suggested that between 3600 B.C. and the present day there have been only 292 years of peace, years without a war of some kind somewhere in the world. He further estimates that in the more than 14,500 wars that have taken place in recorded human history, more than 3.5 billion people have perished, either directly or through war-related famine or epidemic. Thus the war dead come close to equaling the total population of the contemporary world.[13] The twentieth century has certainly not improved on this tragic record. Although we have been increasingly reluctant to use the word war to describe armed conflict within or between nations, whatever they are called, modern wars have been the most numerous and bloody.

Some assumptions that offer justification for war need to be examined. War is seen as contributing a major energizing force to civilization. Despite the destruction it inflicts, war is thought to have generally positive benefits, benefits that outweigh its costs. Another assumption is that war may be a process of natural selection that clears away the obsolete and less desirable aspects of civilization and makes room for better elements to develop. Whatever the assumptions, society's glorification of war communicates, in many cases, an unrestrained enthusiasm for it.

Another attempt to justify war comes from St. Augustine. His just war theory, which is still referenced today, holds that an armed conflict that defends civilization against serious injury is justified. Augustine taught that five principles should guide the decision to go to war: (1) the war is declared by legitimate authority; (2) it is pursued for a just cause; (3) it is fought only as a last resort; (4) it is fought for the right reasons; and (5) it is pursued in a proper manner, that is, without deliberate attack on civilians. Augustine viewed war as the consequence of the imperfect, sinful world in which we live. And as with any other human sin, he attempted to control it, believing that its elimination was impossible.[14] The just war criteria are clearly an attempt to minimize war; they are not a resource for peace.

In the nuclear age we can no longer romanticize war, and we can no longer believe it to be beneficial. Augustine's test is rendered obsolete. In addition to the human costs it exacts, war and its preparation have a powerful dehumanizing effect on people. It has a reciprocal relationship with hate. Elie Wiesel wrote:

> Hate wears many masks. It comes disguised as racial or religious superiority, or it can wear the mask of patriotism or revolution. It is the cancer at the root of human relationships—among individuals and entire nations. But strangely, the phenomenon of hate itself and the evil it fosters has rarely been addressed. Although hate has been with humankind since the beginning—since Cain struck down his brother Abel—it remains an uncharted sickness in the human soul.[15]

Kenneth Boulding notes that "each party in a conflictual relationship is a creation of the enemies. Folly and illusion beget greater folly and illusion and ill will...."[16] Escalation of hate also occurs when war lasts a long time. The families of the casualties feel bound in loyalty to the dead loved one to continue to hate; otherwise it would seem their sons and daughters, brothers and sisters, died in vain. Another terrible cost is the dehumanization that accompanies preparation and participation in combat. As important as the skills learned in basic training are, the system is a deliberate attack on the individuality and free will of the trainees to the end that they will do things they would not be willing to do otherwise. The title of an early anti-nuclear war film, *Dr. Strangelove or How I Learned To Stop Worrying and Love the Bomb,* with its final scene in which the military cowboy astride the just-released nuclear bomb rides it to its destination waving his hat in celebration, or the memorable line from the movie *Apocalypse Now,* "I love the smell of napalm in the morning; it smells like victory," exemplify that suspension of normal moral judgment by people caught up in the frenzy of war.

In support of war, traditional values have been assumed. It is said that war controls population and improves the gene pool through a process of selecting out the strong and eliminating the weak. The research and development for weaponry is believed to produce important technlogical breakthroughs that are useful in peacetime. A war economy is supposed to create high employment and well-paying jobs. The self-discipline and sacrifice that citizens are called on to offer build national character. Victorious societies are thought to be superior to those that are eliminated. And finally, revolutionary war brings moral victory as it enables people to achieve freedom. It is the task of research to subject these assumptions to rigorous scrutiny.[17]

Attempts to identify the causes of war have intrigued scholars, theologians, and many others who believe that if only we could find the source we could eliminate the problem. Wide disagreement exists, and we have come to believe that, like the cancer it is, there is no one single cause of war. Clearly, overpopulation, unequal distribution or scarcity of the world's material resources, political oppression, ignorance, and injustice are major sources of war. The search for justice demands careful investigation of the causes and a creative invention of solutions to the earth's great human and environmental problems. Widespread malnutrition in the Third World appears to be a distribution rather than a production problem. Population appears to be straining the capacity of the earth to support human life and widening the gap between rich and poor countries. The time has come for the most prosperous nations to address, if not the causes, at least the effects of the unequal distribution of the earth's bounty. Challenging questions need to be answered. We need to investigate the limits that should be set for economic growth in the First World; identify a poverty line below which is not acceptable; make birth control available to all; create literacy programs for the Third World; support concurrent economic growth and environmental stewardship; redirect the utilization of resources now being used to fuel military preparation.

The distinguished historian Barbara Tuchman has identified another cause of war: human error or fallibility. In her book *The March of Folly,* she demonstrates through the analysis of case studies that major wars often have resulted from the failure of individual political and military leaders, from ignorance, poor judgment, and emotional instability. The loss of life, material waste, and human pain that resulted from the failure of the individual leader is too enormous to contemplate. [18]

More subtle, but no less powerful, however, are other causes of war that have been hypothesized from the data of psychological investigation. These theories touch the human soul, and may be of first order in correcting the material and political inequities among human beings. They also can be seen as the traditional and perhaps most appropriate province of religion. Three areas of psychological inquiry—social and cognitive psychology, depth psychology, and contemporary research on the human subconscious—contribute some promising research evidence concerning the sources of human violence.

Social and cognitive psychology ask how people perceive other people. Research findings give rise to the suspicion that individuals project on others some of their own traits. For example, the honest person perceives others as honest. Aggressive individuals who have achieved status through cut-throat practices assume others employ the same methods. Limited information about individuals or groups often gives rise to paranoid fantasies. This research postulates that the behavior of individuals closely resembles the behavior of nations. Work in depth psychology reveals a troubling discovery—many people do not necessarily want peace. Inner conflicts manifest themselves externally in a desire for war and destruction. Contemporary research on consciousness reveals that our perceptions, motivations, values, and behavior are shaped by unconscious beliefs. This unconscious programming is extremely powerful and is the foundation for external actions. The sports world has discovered this technique. Coaches encourage athletes to engage in imaging physical skills. The imaging and affirmation of peace can be an effective way to change the perceptions and behaviors of people who might otherwise be disposed to its opposite.[19]

Finally, war creates its own momentum. Our society, for example, can be called with justification a robust war system, self-fueling and self-perpetuating. It can accurately be called a "warfare state," because the share of the U.S. national budget dedicated to defense is still enormous. Claims on our productive capacity, the use of natural resources, and the scientific energy used by the military are so large as to seriously cripple social welfare, the economy, and long-term economic prosperity at home, not to mention the needs of the world's poor abroad.[20]

We can respond in many positive ways to the facts and theories that seem to offer root causes. Robert Jay Lifton urges human beings to explore how to create artistic and cultural icons that communicate the importance and beauty of peace. He believes that the creation of symbols from human experience for the purpose of coming to terms with life is as primary a task for women and men as is eating or moving.[21] Is not one of the major tasks of religion to do just that? Is not one of the purposes of the Temple to do just that?

Not many of us are symbol makers (the poets and artists of society) but other kinds of responses are within our power. If we are ever to reduce or eliminate violence, of whatever scope, we will need to devise a wide variety of responses to its causes. For example, it is astonishing that offenders can go through the whole criminal justice system in this country and never be confronted directly with the misery they have caused. A Victim/Offender Reconciliation Program has been developed in many communities in which the victim and the offender are brought together so the offender has to confront the tragedy of his or her actions for other human beings. This has been an efficacious mechanism for getting offenders to take responsibility for their actions.

On no other issue is the Christian dilemma between theological principle and practical necessity more anguished than on the issue of violence and nonviolence. The Gospels speak eloquently about the love that leads to nonviolence and peace. In light of that proclamation, is there any choice open to the faithful Christian except to refuse to use violence under any circumstances? Many faithful Christians have found other choices, however. Kent Shifferd suggests that three influences account for the legitimate confusion surrounding Christ's teachings on violence. The first is Christianity's inheritance from the Old Testament. That tradition glorified war and depicted Yahweh as the commanding general leading the attack against unbelievers. The second influence is found in the New Testament itself. The teachings of Jesus about love and peace seem clear enough, but they stand in contradiction to statements couched in violent terms that describe his mission. Such statements appear to accept the eschatology of late Palestinian Judaism which anticipated and described the last days in terms of a divine holy war that would finally set things right in the world. Third, the social environment in which Christianity found itself promoted violence against unbelievers. Through the centuries, exclusivity and orthodoxy hardened Christianity into a creedal and legalistic religion. The barriers thus established clearly defined those for whom the grace of God was available and those for whom it was not. Christian practice excluded from God's grace Jews, Muslims, witches, and Christians who rebelled against civil authority (for example, the sixteenth-century peasant revolt in which Luther sided with the oppressive princes).[22]

Jesus was a pacifist, and his followers understood his teachings. It was not until Constantine, early in the fourth century, that the church, moving into closer proximity to the nation, lost its pacifist vision.[23] It is possible, however, that the early Christian rejection of violence was not based on ethical principles but rather on the belief that the end of the world was imminent and that violence was unnecessary. Once Christians had lost faith in an imminent end of time, they saw themselves in permanent residence in the world and began to adjust to its requirements. When service in the Roman army was no longer viewed as service to the gods of Rome, Christians could follow their faith and at the same time engage in military service.[24] Four influential early church fathers—Clement, Tertullian, Origen, and Ambrose—opposed war in general but permitted participation under certain circumstances. Clement believed the Christian could grow spiritually whatever his or her occupation, including military service. Ambrose taught that Christians had a moral obligation to use force to defend another person. "He who does not keep harm off a friend, if he can, is as much in fault as he who causes it."[25]

Christian pacifism and just war doctrine part company over method. Early pacifists practiced withdrawal from society; just war Christians accepted Augustine's belief that human history would move gradually toward peace through the power of God's grace. The requirements of the just war doctrine have had and continue to have the much stronger influence on the Western view of war. Many Christians believe they can be faithful to the Christian tradition and accept the necessity of warfare but should, at the same time, distrust all existing political societies.

In addition to the just war tradition which limits war and the sectarian pacifism of withdrawal from the world, a third tradition finds the cure for discord among nations in the establishment of a new, more universal, and rightly constituted political order. This view sees the possibility of the transformation of the world into a new form of community in which violence and war disappear to make room for a better life for all human beings.[26]

As we have already noted, the tradition of nonviolence is an ancient ethical concept enunciated by Eastern religions and Christianity, as well as by some ancient philosophers who seem to have supported it as a principle without reference to religious belief. Its modern expression in the thought and action of Gandhi and Martin Luther King, Jr., is instructive. Nonviolence is not always successful, nor is it suited to every conflict. Furthermore, it has some serious weaknesses as well as outstanding strengths. It is a method that many Westerners find alien even though it has been used successfully in the United States, most notably by the Civil Rights movement.

John Dear defines nonviolent resistance as

> the willingness to take on suffering ourselves in order to right wrongs, in order to change the evil system of death that is all around us into freedom and life and love for everyone....Nonviolent resistance is an act of liberation from our enslavement to violence and injustice, into the freedom of life in the spirit of God—the life of love and truth.[27]

Martin Luther King, Jr., noted that civil disobedience was a last resort, to be used only when all other means of redress of legitimate grievances have been tried and failed. The first step of the process is to identify the injustice by attempting to raise the consciousness of society. Only after that effort has failed to mobilize the power structure to change does civil disobedience, or noncooperation with the existing system, become a duty.[28]

Finding his inspiration in Hinduism, Christianity, and the American transcendentalist, Henry David Thoreau, Mohandas K. Gandhi developed an ethic and a strategy that freed India from British colonialism. Gandhi enunciated the concept of *satyagraha* (*satya* standing for truth which is equated with love and *graha* signifying force). The concept is literally translated "truth force" or "love force." Its English rendering as "passive resistance" is misleading. *Satyagraha* is active and assertive; it requires great energy and courage; and it endeavors to persuade the opponent that it is better to eliminate the sources of the conflict than for either side to be defeated or annihilated. Furthermore, Gandhi rejected absolutely any argument that proposed that ends justify means. He taught that there was "the same inviolable connection between the means and the end as there is between the seed and the tree." The rigorous discipline of nonviolent resistance permitted anger and hatred but recommended that these feelings be directed toward the system of evil and not toward individuals. Love was the guiding principle for all strategy and behavior. Gandhi noted pragmatically that if the biblical injunction "an eye for an eye, a tooth for a tooth" were followed, the whole world would be blind and toothless. He saw nonviolence as proactive and its goal as the transformation of the opponent, helping him or her become aware of the evil present in society. King continuously reminded his followers that they would have to bear the brunt of the suffering:

> Every time I see [hate] I say to myself, hate is too great a burden to bear. Somehow we must be able to stand up before our most bitter opponents and say: "We shall match your capacity to inflict suffering by our capacity to endure suffering. We will meet your physical force with soul force. Do to us what you will and we will still love....Be assured that we will wear you down by our capacity to suffer, and one day we will win our freedom."[29]

Finally, nonviolent civil disobedience provides for the right of the individual to choose his or her course of action and at the same time acknowledge society's right to exact the consequences of that choice. Thus participants in nonviolent protest expected and accepted punishment and loss of privileges.

I will never forget the faculty meeting called by President James Nabrit in the fall of 1962 at Texas Southern University (at that time the State University for Negroes) where I was on the faculty. He knew before many of us that the Civil Rights movement would reach Houston during that school year and that our students would be involved. He appealed to each of us to offer advice and support to our students whatever choice they were considering, but he did not prescribe what kind of counsel we should offer. He informed us, however, that we needed to know and communicate to our students that any person convicted of a felony in Texas could never receive a license to teach or practice law or medicine. That would be the consequence for students majoring in those fields who would later that year integrate lunch counters and movie theaters and be beaten, jailed, and convicted. I have often wondered what happened to those brave young people.

John Henry Yoder, the Mennonite authority on nonviolence, has developed a topology of pacifism that exhaustively describes its many variations. He discusses no less than eighteen different types, each springing from its own root. Yoder believes that to lump them all together under the heading of pacifism is to do them a grave injustice. Six variants deserve special consideration. First, the pacifism of the honest study of cases is a selective response to a given situation. By rigorously examining each situation the individual assesses his or her ability to participate in the existing system or decides to oppose it. Second is the opposite stance, the pacifism of absolute principle, in which the individual applies a principle consistently in every situation. For example, a person would not kill another person under any circumstances. Third, the pacifism of programmatic political alternatives seeks means other than war to solve the problems of international relations. Fourth, the pacifism of nonviolent social change is exemplified by the Indian movement for independence and the American Civil Rights movement. Fifth, the pacifism of prophetic protest assumes a disruptive mode. Destroying draft records, violating anti-protest statutes outside nuclear plants or abortion clinics are examples. Sixth, the pacifism of proclamation is not limited by what is thought to be possible of realization. It takes as its standard its understanding of Jesus' ministry and affirms that the kingdom of God is at hand, brought into being by divine grace and human response. Proclamation is not exclusively for the objective of baptism but is a message of peace and justice for all human beings.[30]

Because the means are so important to the practitioner of nonviolence, they received special attention from the leadership of any nonviolent effort. I remember that fall at Texas Southern a conversation with a student who showed me a copy of the instructions given to each person who planned to participate in nonviolent protest. I understood then as I had not before how the movement had achieved such strong discipline in the face of violent attack. The code of conduct I saw contained the following points: (1) maintain an attitude of goodwill at all times; (2) avoid malicious language, slogans, or labels to stigmatize or ridicule the opponent; (3) if force or violence is used against you, your teammates, or others, do not retaliate; never use violence; (4) do not carry weapons of any kind or implements that could be used or interpreted as weapons, such as a pocketknife; (5) abide by decisions of the group or, when in action, follow orders given by the authorized group leader, and avoid maverick behavior; (6) without abrogating the above, exercise creative judgment and initiative, and be flexible, willing to experiment; (7) be ready to assume leadership of the team if required to do so; (8) submit to arrest promptly and politely unless a policy of noncooperation has been decided on; (9) be punctual and precise in carrying out all tasks; (10) maintain a neat appearance and dignified posture at all times in conformity with the moral image of the cause, which includes speaking simply, clearly, and to the point and avoiding tendentiousness, and being prepared to give a straightforward reply to relevant questions as well as to ignore with good grace any inflammatory remarks, jeers or other verbal abuse from the opponent. These would not be easy instructions to follow in the presence of violence and brutality.

Powerful images of the civil rights struggle haunt our collective memories: police dogs, fire hoses, an earthen dam grave, a multitude gathered in front of the Lincoln Memorial. For me, one unforgettable moment was a television story of a group of protesters kneeling in front of (but not blocking) the entrance to the Dizzyland Diner in a small Southern community. Frustrated beyond endurance, the proprietor came out with an egg in his hand and broke it on the head of one of the young men. A week later the proprietor was interviewed on television. He had seen the tape of his action and with tears running down his face he said, "I am so ashamed. I will never do that again." A mirror had been held up before the face of his hatred and he could not stand to see it.

Variations have succeeded elsewhere in recent history. Although predominantly, but not completely, nonviolent, popular uprisings in the Philippines, South Korea, and several countries in eastern Europe, notably Poland and the former Czechoslovakia, have accomplished revolutionary changes with nonviolent methods. Those who support civil disobedience of whatever kind believe it is equally effective in dealing with conflict within a family or local community as it is within a nation. In fact, Gandhi credits his wife with helping him see its potential as she modeled it in their marriage in response to his dictatorial and domineering behavior.[31]

Both Gandhi and Martin Luther King, Jr., recognized violence as a demonic force. They resisted an evil society using peaceful methods as vigorously as others might use force. They resisted with love for the enemy instead of hate, believing that a transformation of the human heart was possible and that the sum of violence in the world could be reduced by courageous, nonviolent action.[32]

Several years ago, then-U.S. Surgeon General C. Everett Koop listed the fifteen most serious public health problems in the United States. One of those was violence. He directed the Centers for Disease Control to begin to study violence as it studies any epidemic—gathering statistics, identifying groups most at risk, and assessing promising interventions. As valuable as this effort may be, our Christian discipleship should suggest a different approach. We are called to take a stand against violence. We can model peaceful behaviors, affirm peaceful achievements, participate in organizations that make peace, and pray for God's Spirit to bless and guide the efforts of all peacemakers.

## Notes

1. Hannah Arendt, *On Violence* (New York: Harcourt, Brace & World, 1969), 80.
2. David Gelman, "The Violence in Our Heads," *Newsweek* (August 2, 1993): 48.
3. "Navajo Code Talkers: A Few Good Men, *Smithsonian* vol. 24 (August 1993): 42.
4. Jimmy Carter, *Talking Peace: A Vision for the Next Generation* (New York: Dutton's Children's Books, 1993), 158–159.
5. Konrad Lorenz, *On Aggression*, trans. Marjorie Wilson (New York: Harcourt, Brace & World, 1974), 299.
6. Irenaus Eibl-Eibesfeldt, *Love and Hate: The Natural History of Behavior Patterns* (New York: Holt, Rinehart & Winston, 1971), 245–246.
7. David P. Barash, *Introduction to Peace Studies* (Belmont, California: Wadsworth Publishing, 1991), 138ff.
8. J. Glenn Gray, *The Warriors: Reflections on Men in Battle* (New York: Harcourt, Brace & Co., 1959).
9. Myriam Miedzian, *Boys Will Be Boys: Breaking the Link Between Masculinity and Violence* (New York: Doubleday, 1991).
10. G. Clarke Chapman, "Approaching Nuclearism as a Heresy," in Ira Chernus and Edward Linenthal, eds., *A Shuddering Dawn: Religious Studies and the Nuclear Age* (Albany, New York: State University of New York Press, 1989), 95–101.
11. Walter Wink, *Engaging the Powers: Discernment and Resistance in a World of Domination* (Minneapolis, Minnesota: Augsburg Fortress, 1992), 13–31.
12. Elise Boulding, "The Child and Nonviolent Social Change," *Handbook on Peace Education*, Christoph Wulf, ed. (International Peace Research Association, 1974), 101–132.

13. Quoted by Francis Beer, *Peace Against War: The Ecology of International Violence* (San Francisco: W.H. Freeman and Company, 1981), 20.
14. Glen H. Stassen, *Just Peacemaking: Transforming Initiatives for Justice and Peace* (Louisville, Kentucky: Westminster/John Knox Press, 1992), 232–233.
15. Elie Wiesel, "Anatomy of Hate: Resolving Conflict through Dialogue and Democracy," Aug. 26–29, 1990, Elie Wiesel Foundation for Humanity, Oslo, Norway, page 1 (cover).
16. Kenneth Boulding, *Stable Peace* (Austin, Texas: University of Texas Press, 1978), 3–30.
17. Ronald J. Glossop, "Confronting War," in *Dilemmas of War and Peace: A Source Book*, Dick Ringler, ed. (Board of Regents of the University of Wisconsin System and the Corporation for Public Broadcasting), 1993, 116–117.
18. Barbara Tuchman, *The March of Folly* (New York: Ballantine Books, 1985).
19. Richard Smoke and Willis Harmon, "Paths to Peace," in *Dilemmas of War and Peace: A Source Book*, Dick Ringler, ed. (Board of Regents of the University of Wisconsin System and the Corporation for Public Broadcasting, 1993), 195–197.
20. Thomas Keefe and Ron E. Roberts, *Realizing Peace: An Introduction to Peace Studies* (Ames, Iowa: Iowa State University Press, 1991), 104.
21. Robert Jay Lifton, *History and Human Survival* (New York: Random House, 1961), 248.
22. Kent Shifferd, "Theses On Christian Violence," *Transactions of the Wisconsin Academy of Sciences, Arts & Letters*, 71, part 2 (1983): 60–77.
23. James Turner Johnson, *The Quest for Peace: Three Moral Traditions in Western Cultural History* (Princeton, New Jersey: Princeton University Press, 1987).
24. David G. Hunter, "A Decade of Research on Early Christians and Military Service," *Religious Studies Review* 18 (April 1992): 87–94.
25. Ibid., 87–89.
26. James Turner Johnson, *The Quest for Peace*.
27. John Dear, *Our God Is Nonviolent: Witnesses in the Struggle for Peace & Justice* (New York: The Pilgrim Press, 1990), 7–11.
28. Martin Luther King, Jr., *Why We Can't Wait* (New York: New American Library, 1964).
29. Quoted in Coretta Scott King, ed., *The Words of Martin Luther King, Jr.* (New York: Newmarket Press, 1983), 79.
30. John H. Yoder, *Nevertheless: The Varieties and Shortcomings of Religious Pacifism* (Scottsdale, Pennsylvania: Herald Press, 1971).

31. "Gandhi Marg," *Journal of the Gandhi Peace Foundation* 11, no. 2 (July-September 1989): 133–143; and M.K. Gandhi, *An Autobiography: The Story of My Experience With Truth* (Ahmidabad, India: Navajivan, 1989).
32. Richard Gregg, *The Power of Nonviolence* (London: James Clarke, 1960).

# The Global Family

Several years ago, I had the pleasure of choosing a gift for the outgoing president of the Iowa Peace Institute. I found a globe of the world that showed the land masses of this planet as they appear from space—there were no political boundaries. It was an appropriate symbol for a man who had worked locally and internationally to eliminate the divisions that separate and alienate human beings.

The present system of nation-states came into being in 1648 with the Peace of Westphalia, which ended the Thirty Years War in Europe, a war that had decimated a third of the population of the participants. The basic assumption that has defined the thinking of people ever since has been that the world order is and ought to be composed exclusively of sovereign states. This theory holds that governments are sovereign and equal and that they will act in their own best interest. No higher power can or should claim authority. This assumption does not describe reality. Nations are not equal in land, or in human or economic resources. In fact, since 1648 some nations have consolidated so much power that they have been able to control vast areas of the world that are not contiguous or even close geographically to their seat of power—the phenomenon of colonialism. Clearly there is no real balance of power that holds all nations in equilibrium. This "Wesphalian logic" has not been able to alleviate poverty, hunger, and misery, or protect human rights or the environment. And it certainly has not been able to eliminate the arms race or prevent war. For example, neither China nor France agreed to the Limited Test Ban Treaty of 1963, which was successfully negotiated between the United States and the Soviet Union. In 1993 after thirty test-free years worldwide, China detonated a nuclear device and France in retaliation threatened to follow suit. "It is very difficult to escape the conclusion that the logic of Westphalia now seems unable to protect the most vital needs of most of humanity."[1]

What in 1648 was a new world order has become in our day the old world order. The nation-state may not be the end point of political evolution but only a way station on the road toward a more mature world order. From the clan to the tribe, from larger geographic entities to empire, from loyalty for emperor to allegiance for nation, human beings have been struggling to resolve the problem of living together. At the same time, the effect of war has grown exponentially. "With Napoleon, limited war gave way to total war. Technology provided breech-loading rifles, long-range, large-caliber artillery, and the machine guns. The railroad and the truck made it possible to fight year round."[2] The scientific genius of our own age has given us weapons of unthinkable accuracy and long-distance destructive power.

The diplomats who negotiated the Peace of Westphalia could not have imagined in their wildest dreams the interdependency of the modern world. In economics, for example, interest rates in Germany affect the strength of the U.S. dollar, and the number of cars manufactured in Japan impact employment in Lamoni, Iowa, as well as in Detroit. As the Third World debtor nations began to default and restructure their enormous debt, funded in part by major U.S. banks, our economic interdependence became even more apparent. On the positive side, investment is no longer pursued exclusively within national borders. Obviously we belong to a much larger economic entity than our own nation.

With this growing economic interdependence has come a corresponding struggle to achieve stronger international law. The term "international law" was first used by Jeremy Bentham in 1783 in his book *Principles of International Law.* It inherited its foundation and assumptions from Dutch legal scholar Hugo Grotius in his 1625 book entitled *On the Law of War and Peace.*[3] It has only been during the last fifty years, however, that significant progress has been made toward the growth of international law.

One important pillar of existing international law is custom. The immunity of diplomats, for example, is honored by long-standing practice. A second pillar is the "common heritage of mankind." This concept has recently provided the basis for discussions about international resources such as the ocean bed, Antarctica, and the ozone layer of the earth's atmosphere, all of which transcend national sovereignty and affect human life and well-being. International treaties are a third pillar. Recent years have seen an unusual proliferation. The United Nations has registered 18,000 international treaties, as many as were concluded in the preceding 2,000 years. Since 1945 the documents contained in the 900 volumes of the U.N. Treaty Series have more than doubled the number of treaties signed, from the

Peace of Westphalia in 1648 to the closing of the League of Nations in 1945.

Another pillar of international law is the existence of a system of international courts. Established in 1908, the Central American Court of Justice existed for only ten years. The new Inter-American Court of Human Rights located in Costa Rica is now serving Central America. The European Court of Justice has authority in the Common Market nations as does the European Court of Human Rights. These two courts have begun to accumulate a body of substantive and procedural European case law based on provisions of operative treaties. Best known among international judicial bodies is the International Court of Justice located at The Hague. Its decisions are authoritative, but there is no mechanism for enforcement. They have been disregarded often by even those nations that participate in its proceedings, including the United States.

Still another pillar of international law deals with war. Provisions for control are, of course, difficult to draw up and, at the present time, impossible to enforce. The Nuremberg Principles, however, did attempt to codify behavior of combatants. The principles described crimes against the peace, in which wars of aggression in violation of treaties are initiated; crimes against humanity, which include murder, extermination, enslavement, deportation, and other inhuman acts committed against civilians; and finally war crimes, which include ill-treatment of prisoners of war, killing of hostages, plunder of property, and wanton destruction not justified militarily.[4]

As the world becomes more interconnected, the need for stronger international law becomes more apparent. We need better laws of the sea, the skies, the land and forests, energy resources, industry and agriculture, credit and finance, and, finally, laws of arms and aggression. In a world undergoing enormous change, important developments are possible. The United Nations Charter effected historic achievements in the areas of the prohibition of unauthorized use of force and the protection of fundamental human rights. However, with persuasive powers but no enforcement mechanisms this progress is limited.[5]

Harold Lasswell projects two extreme scenarios for future possibilities in the development of international law. His most optimistic projection describes a wider and more responsible sharing of power and a greater protection of and wider acknowledgment of the values of human dignity among the peoples of the world. His most pessimistic scenario sees a retreat to more isolated political units, authoritarian in nature and ruled by a military elite.[6] This construct is based on the assumption that many of the world's political leaders will pursue special interests without acknowledging the common problems of global humanity. As more people become aware of the compelling self-interest that would be served by enforceable international statutes, such statutes might come into being. It is apparent that, in the words of Benjamin Ferencz and Ken Keyes, Jr., "We must replace the law of force with the force of law."[7]

Recent demonstrations of the unilateral abuse of power by political leaders have caused many people to come to the conclusion that some authority transcending that of the nation state needs to be established. An early response to this felt need was the first Geneva Convention, held in 1864. Two peace conferences held at The Hague in 1899 and 1907 attempted to lay down rules that would ensure neutrality, condemn aggression, encourage nonviolent efforts to resolve international conflicts, and, when all else failed, require a formal declaration of war. The League of Nations was more successful than many people believe. It helped settle almost half of the disputes it considered. These were minor disputes, however, and it failed to impact the major ones which were the precursors of World War II. Doomed from the beginning by its severe limitations and by the failure of the United States to participate, the League worked for a reduction and limitation of armaments. Ironically the first arms limitation conference was held under League auspices in 1932 just as Adolph Hitler was setting in motion the greatest military buildup ever undertaken. The League's only lasting achievement may be its role as a forerunner to the establishment of the United Nations. Its existence and operation provided a precedent for a transnational parliament which to that time had been only an ideal, and it created a basis on which later efforts could be made.

Still in effect today, but of limited effectiveness, was the 1928 General Treaty for the Renunciation of War, popularly called the Kellogg-Briand Pact or the Pact of Paris. Its provisions are entirely consistent with the U.N. Charter, and it was cited in 1973 when Australia complained to the International Court of Justice against the French nuclear tests in the South Pacific.[8]

Since 1945 the United Nations has been an important presence in the world. The U.N. was not unanimously welcomed in this country. Not too long ago, billboards reading "Get the U.S. Out of the U.N." dotted the nation's highways. Its general effectiveness has been a matter of serious debate. It has been accused of perpetuating in its charter a Westphalian logic—the supreme nation state will brook no external interference with its behavior. Hampered by a small budget and little legal authority, the present structure of the U.N. may not be appropriate for the post cold war world. Despite these disabilities, however, the U.N. has achieved some remarkable accomplishments. Its documents have enunciated a primitive vision of a new system of world order based on a concert of nations.

From its vantage point, the U.N. has become sensitive to global needs and has found ways to promulgate them. For example, the U.N. has gathered the most extensive body of data describing the human family ever accumulated, such as distribution of population, age groups, numbers of handicapped and malnourished, illiteracy rates, life expectancies, etc. The U.N. has facilitated conferences on economic development, world population, youth, aging, women, racism. It has provided a forum in which Third World countries could articulate their claims for justice and express their points of view. More specifically, it has assisted 1 billion people to gain independence from colonial powers. It can point to concrete gains in economic well-being and human rights in a number of poorer countries. It has provided a platform on which the superpowers could pound their shoes and otherwise vent their frustrations with each other during the most tense moments of the cold war. Its peacekeeping missions have maintained stability when larger scale war threatened—in the Gaza Strip, at the Suez Canal, in Cyprus, at the Israeli-Jordanian border, in the Congo, at the India-Pakistani border. It supervised the establishment of independence in Namibia, the withdrawal of Soviet troops from Afghanistan, a solution in Cambodia, the end of the Iran-Iraq War, the beginning of the end of apartheid in South Africa, and the pacification of southern Lebanon. The good offices of the secretary general helped win the release of U.S. hostages from Iran.[9]

Special credit should be given to the Canadian troops who have played an important role in many of these achievements and to former Canadian Prime Minister Lester Pearson, who was awarded a Nobel Peace Prize. The failures of the U.N. have underscored the limitations under which it operates. Sensitive to the criticisms of the inadequacy of their efforts in the former Yugoslavia, for example, one Canadian commander noted that by the time the U.N. peacekeeping force arrived "there was no peace to keep."[10] Old ways of thinking, ways made obsolete by the existence of nuclear power and environmental degradation, should not prevent people from supporting the U.N. Individuals do not have to give up their cherished national loyalties to reduce dangerous international chaos.[11]

One of the U.N.'s grandest achievements is the bold stand on human rights contained in its documents. The discovery of the atrocities against people committed by the Third Reich during World War II shocked the world. Since that time human rights has received major attention. The concept has evolved slowly in human history. Human rights ideals were not unknown in the ancient world. The world's religions all taught compassion in treatment of human beings. For Judaism and Islam the basis for compassion was not so much that people had a right to such treatment but rather that the givers owed it as a duty to God. Christianity emphasized inherent or natural rights, which no doubt provided the basis for subsequent secular theories. Often, however, religious obligation was used to justify brutal treatment by today's standards.[12]

As national sovereignty came into being worldwide in the mid-seventeenth century, governments agreed to ignore the treatment of people within other countries as none of their business. At the same time, the Enlightenment promoted the idea of intrinsic human rights, stemming from natural order. This view holds that government has no authority to create these rights, but must recognize them, existing as they do independent of society. Government does have, however, an obligation to protect them.[12] And finally, and much later, the human rights record of a given nation can be scrutinized and criticized by the rest of the world. It was apparently its poor human rights record more than any other factor that caused China to lose its bid to host the Olympic Games in the year 2000. The United States government, at least in part, withholds most favored nation trade status on the basis of a nation's poor human rights record.[13]

Thus the history of human rights progress contains three important elements: first, the acceptance of the basic premise of inherency; second, the delineation of human rights; and third, the awareness and criticism of violations wherever they occur. The first, inalienable human rights for all persons, in Thomas Jefferson's phrase, is not a given in all political ideologies. Marxism, for example, holds that individual rights do not exist unless they are explicitly granted by society. Religious practices sometimes do not recognize human rights; for example, the contemporary suppression of the rights of women by Islamic fundamentalists and the Hindu practice of *suttee* (the burning alive of the widow on her husband's funeral pyre). The second, the definition of what these rights are, continues to be debated. The traditional emphasis in the United States has been on equal civil and political rights with freedom for economic competition. Elsewhere a higher priority has given to every human being the right to a minimum socioeconomic standard.

These two groups of rights are often in conflict, and countries have found it necessary to establish priorities. For example, the Marxist emphasis on socioeconomic rights restricts civil and political freedoms which are seen as endangering these rights. In general, the so-called First World (the developed capitalist states) see human rights in terms of civil, political, and economic freedoms. The Second and Third Worlds (the centrally planned economies and the impoverished states respectively) emphasize human rights in terms of socioeconomic guarantees. The right to housing and employment, to education, to medical care and old age security, no matter how meager, loom large in less affluent societies.[14]

Article 55 of the United Nations Charter provided the world with a vision of the modern struggle for universal human rights:

> With a view to the creation of conditions of stability and well-being which are necessary for peaceful and friendly relations among nations based on respect for the principle of equal rights and self-determination of peoples, the United Nations shall promote: (a) a higher standard of living, full employment, and conditions of economic and social progress and development; (b) solutions of international economic, social, health, and related problems, and international cultural and educational cooperation; and (c) universal respect for and observance of human rights and fundamental freedoms for all without distinction as to race, sex, language, or religion.

To add flesh to this skeleton, the "Universal Declaration of Human Rights" was adopted unanimously in

1948, with leadership coming primarily from Eleanor Roosevelt. It was an unprecedented action—forty-eight nations agreeing to acknowledge rights and freedoms of the world's peoples. Its basic thesis states that "All human beings are born free and equal in dignity and rights. They are endowed with reason and conscience and should act towards one another in a spirit of brotherhood." Its thirty articles recommend civil, political, socioeconomic, and cultural rights. The document is divided into three parts: a Declaration, a Covenant, and machinery for implementation. The Declaration is a statement of principles. The Covenant spells out specific objectives. Not legally binding, it has had tremendous impact, however, in focusing the world's attention on human rights violations and has, in the view of some judicial scholars, the force of law. Many legal instruments have been based on the Charter and the Declaration. Some of these condemn genocide and racial discrimination. The Geneva Conventions, laying down protocols for armed conflict, have been expanded as part of this general process of fine tuning. The European Court of Human Rights and the Inter-American Commission for Human Rights are both responses to this heightened awareness. In 1975 the Helsinki Accord called for a freer flow of ideas across borders, for the reuniting of families separated by East-West conflict, and for renewed effort to protect human rights in the thirty-five signatory nations. Undoubtedly and ironically this agreement hastened the demise of communism. Inspired by the ideals expressed in these documents, a number of independent organizations as well as U.N. agencies monitor the status of human rights around the world: The U.N. Human Rights Commission, the International Labor Organization, UNESCO,

UNICEF, WHO, the High Commission on Refugees, Amnesty International, the International Red Cross, and the International Red Crescent.[15]

Although the human rights record of the United States is far from perfect, we can take pride in the world leadership we have offered. In his final public statement as president, Jimmy Carter reminded us of our heritage: "America did not invent human rights. In a very real sense, it was the other way around. Human rights invented America. We were the first nation in the world to be founded on such an idea."[16] Rather than making us complacent, that heritage should motivate us to even greater effort to assure human rights at home.

What is the future of the nation-state in a world that has been brought so close together by transportation, communication, and a host of pressing problems? The power and importance of nationalism to human beings is extremely important. Piaget and Weil observed that "the child's discovery of his homeland...[is part of a broader] process of transition from egocentricity to reciprocity...." However, they also noted that this human phenomenon can include groups either smaller or larger than the child's own country.[17] We know that cultural inheritance, which is often territorial and political, supports important values. The celebration of common experience, the enjoyment of known and understood relations with other group members, and the desire to perpetuate these values into the next generation have all proved to be important in the lives of the world's peoples, so important in fact that people have been willing to die to preserve them.[18] Human continuity is supported by a sense of belonging to a geographical/racial/cultural group. The root of the word "nation" is the same as that of "origin" or "birth."[19] Often, at least in Western societies, "shared information, affection, and habits of compromise, tolerance, and trust provide a basis for maintaining peace."[20] It is no mystery, then, that the introduction of a global curriculum often brings angry citizens to school board meetings, as happened in Iowa a few years ago.

The arguments in opposition to global curricula appear to grow out of a "scarcity" assumption. If we acknowledge the value of other countries, or other cultures, or other religions, we have somehow devalued our own country, culture, or religion. It is as if there is only so much value in the world and, if we share it, then we have less for ourselves. We need to develop the attitude that when we recognize value in others we have truly enriched ourselves.[21]

The international dilemmas facing human beings have become so great as to require new ways of doing business if global problems are to be solved and peace is to be achieved. Those who insist that absolute national sovereignty be maintained must accept the burden of proof to explain how the critical global problems we face can be solved by the status quo. Every American president since Harry Truman has acknowledged the need for some sort of world order change that would help solve the problems that affect all human beings. For example, George Bush noted, "Our aim [must be] to take the lead in forging peace and freedom's best hope, a great and growing commonwealth of free nations."[22] The leaders of many other nations have agreed with the principle but not with the mechanism. Speaking at Fulton, Missouri, on May 6, 1992, Mikhail Gorbachev called for a global government with power to halt international conflict, to avoid ecological disaster, and to provide the good life to more and more human beings on the planet. "On today's agenda is not just a union of democratically organized states, but also a democratically organized world community."[23]

When there is such unanimity for change among national leaders—those people who have the broadest views of the problems besetting our world—we surely must pay attention. The inability of the sovereign-state system to control both the creation and distribution of armaments is self-evident. Added to the danger of war is the unavailability of the money spent on arms to alleviate the physical deprivation of a large part of humanity. Archbishop Desmond Tutu estimates that almost a thousand billion dollars are expended each year worldwide on arms and armed forces. This is more than the poorer half of humanity earns. In a world where one person out of every five lives in absolute poverty, this reality is more than absurd, more than tragic.[24] It is unimaginably sinful. And our present world organization has been able to do very little about it.

Less apparent but no less dangerous is the ecological threat to the entire planet which cries out for some international management. Jacques Cousteau proposes a terrifying scenario. What if one poor nation agrees, for a substantial monetary payment, to become the depository for another nation's nuclear waste? The nuclear waste must be transported by ship. Because no international regulations exist, the donor nation ships the material in a single-hull vessel to save money. The vessel springs a leak discharging radioactive contaminants into the ocean. This would be an international disaster of unimaginable magnitude, and it could happen.[25] Destruction of the world's rain forests, $CO_2$ emissions, and acid rain are all problems that are not contained within national boundaries. They cry out for regulation. Worldwide health epidemics such as AIDS, international terrorism, and drug trafficking require international policy and action for containment. A multiplicity of issues exist that cannot be solved by the current system. Finally, and perhaps most serious, is the great disparity between the rich and poor in this world, which is an issue of justice as well as of law. The billions spent on armaments could be redirected by a supranational authority to secure a basic level of subsistence for every human being.

A variety of terms have been used to label a new kind of worldwide structure: extra- or inter-governmental organization, supranationalism, universalism, transnationalism, holistic global order, commonwealth of nations. These terms have not been precisely defined. Three major idea groups represent the best thinking to date. The first is a plan developed by legal scholars Grenville Clark and Louis Sohn. It proposes that the U.N. become a world peacekeeping power and that, except for disarmament and war, nations would retain their sovereign powers.[26]

The second is a group of ideas proposed by the World Order Model Project (WOMP). One idea is an enhanced state system. All colonial and racist regimes would be outlawed. The U.N. would take on a more significant role, and specialized international agencies would expand and acquire greater power. Greater regional cooperation would be encouraged. The present problems of sovereignty would not be solved by this plan. Another idea is a system of world government. This central authority would control disarmament, monitor competition among smaller political units, regulate environmental practices, and guarantee human rights. Even if it were attainable, this system might not be desirable because of the inherent wastefulness and inefficiency of large bureaucracy.

The third idea of the WOMP group is a regionalist network of power and authority. Using the European Community as a model, this proposal replicates it in other areas of the world as a compromise between national sovereignty on the one hand and world government on the other extreme. Its danger is, of course, that one network would dominate others and use its power to exacerbate present inequalities. In fact, one of the arguments used to support the North American Free Trade Agreement between the United States, Canada, and Mexico is the fear that without a united economic system, this hemisphere will be at a disadvantage in competition with the European Community.

The fourth idea is a power/authority network based on a concert of principal actors. This system would include a formal structure of treaty obligations, an established headquarters site, periodic meetings, and institutional machinery for contact between the principal actors. This form is close to the role of an expanded U.N.

The fifth idea is a "condominium" network of power and authority. Condominium is defined as a cooperative arrangement among the major powers to act together on key world order issues in accord with preset procedures. The problems of identifying the superpowers and maintaining discipline based on the preset procedures are apparent. These five systems are illustrative of the variety of ideas presented by WOMP.[27]

The third major idea that may hold promise is a federalist system modeled on the experience of the United States. Carl Van Doren reminds us that the thirteen original colonies, each with its own parochial interests and a much more diverse population than historians had originally assumed, agreed reluctantly to combine in confederation. They were unwilling to give up important powers to that system. The Confederation did not work, and the federal state was born. The legacy of the American achievement might well be a global federation.[28] Supported by instant communication, this system would, as Strobe Talbott has noted, provide for "a devolution of power not only upward toward supranational bodies and outward toward commonwealths and common markets but also downward toward freer, more autonomous units of administration that permit distinct societies to preserve their cultural identities and govern themselves as much as possible."[29]

Opponents of this concept maintain that the thirteen colonies were much more homogeneous than the world, which made the task of unification easier, and that, more important, this nation had to fight a bloody civil war before the unification was finally permanent. The experience of other nations, however, demonstrates that differences need not divide. Switzerland is made up of four nationalities with four different languages (French, German, Italian, Romansh), crowded geographically into an area much smaller than the old Yugoslavia. The success of the one and the failure of the other may quite possibly be explained by the presence of democracy in Switzerland and its absence in Yugoslavia. A multinational federal state may well hold the solution to the most difficult challenge of divising a world order system that will solve the international problems that face us and at the same time preserve a sense of national identity.

Although the need for some form of world order is tragically evident and the barriers to its accomplishment are daunting, there is some basis for hope. A great deal of technical cooperation is already occurring. Exchanges of industrial and agricultural knowledge are improving conditions in the Second and Third Worlds. After the Chernobyl disaster, for example, an international body of nuclear physicists and technicians have begun to monitor the safety of all accessible nuclear power stations. The International Bank and the International Monetary Fund, even though they have limited their support to non-Communist nations in the past, show signs of expanding their focus of support.[30] Sponsored by the U.N., three international commissions have dealt with four major problems facing the world: The Brandt Report, entitled "North-South: A Program for Survival," recommends that a global energy research center be created and urges the reform of the international monetary system; The Palme Report, entitled "Common Security—A Blueprint for Survival" recommends the strengthening of the peacekeeping capacity of the U.N.; and The Bruntland Report, entitled "Our Common Future," addresses the worldwide environmental crisis.[31]

On October 4, 1993, the German Parliament, the last of the nations of the European Community to do so, approved the Maastricht Treaty. The treaty provides the framework for economic and monetary unity in the European Community, an unprecedented voluntary willingness on the part of twelve countries to give up significant national powers to a supranational entity. Not surprisingly, the ratification process took a long time. The treaty had to be submitted to referendum several times before it passed in one country; it almost brought down the government in another. Its passage, contingent on amendments in at least one country, contains large enough loopholes to allow bailout. After two agonizing years, however, it is finally in force among countries whose ancient animosities have for centuries erupted into recurring warfare.

The creation of the European Community is a tremendous achievement. Not only will there be a common currency (the ECU or European Currency Unit), there is already a common passport. Its flag is twelve gold stars on a field of blue, and its "national" anthem is Beethoven/Schiller's "Ode to Joy." The hope of those who have worked so hard for so long to create the European Community is that this unity will give not only a competitive economic edge in global commerce to its members but that it will also bring down the curtain on centuries of warfare on the European continent.[32]

Another source of hope is the individual pursuit of peace undertaken by thousands of private citizens. Across the world people are joining their efforts in behalf of peace. Currently 18,000 International Non-Governmental Organizations, globe-spanning associations of private citizens, represent a grassroots phenomenon that reflects a universal passion for peace. These organizations vary widely in character and purpose and are united only by their desire for world peace. Each INGO chooses its own agenda and acts out of its own mission. It is impossible to summarize the myriad activities in which they have engaged, but five general categories represent a large part of their activities: lobbying for constructive foreign policies of nation-states; providing education for world citizenship; expanding conceptual innovations and expertise; creating opportunities for the North to learn from the South; and offering activity as an antidote to despair.[33] Special accreditation may be achieved by some of these organizations through application of the INGO to the Department of International Economic and Social Affairs of the U.N. This documentation allows the Economic and Social Council and the Secretariat of the U.N. to engage in consultations with INGOs that are concerned with matters within their interest and authority.

Multi-track diplomacy is another activity undertaken by small groups of private citizens, which has had some success in defusing tense international situations and in the prevention of others. It takes a systems approach to conflict resolution and peacebuilding. It focuses on activities of (1) relationship-building, which assumes that any formal peace settlement must be supplemented by personal and intergroup relationships built on trust, respect, and creative cooperation; (2) consultation, which helps local people create peace systems that make sense for them; (3) training, which provides tools and skills that support indigenous cultural values and methods of the people involved; (4) communication, which guides people in listening to and learning from one another; and (5) education, which provides a variety of ways people can learn about the resolution and transformation of conflict and about peacebuilding.[34]

Yet another basis for hope is found in the leadership that religions of the world are beginning to offer. In August 1993 an important ecumenical event took place. Meeting in Chicago, the Parliament of the World's Religions issued an unprecedented declaration of global ethics to guide human behavior. Representatives of Buddhism, Christianity, Hinduism, Judaism, and 120 other religious groups reached an agreement in principle on a statement of global ethics. The Parliament appealed to those religions that wage war to rise above "mutual arrogance, mistrust, prejudice...and hostility." The conference recommended the development of a global consciousness and confessed the shortcomings of religious practice. "Religion is often misused for purely power-political goals, including war." The Declaration also affirmed, however, that the religious wisdom of the ages, although not speaking directly to modern problems, has much to offer the world. Although the signatories did not bind their religious groups, many prominent religious leaders added their support to the document whose principal author was Swiss theologian Hans Küng. The Declaration articulates a minimal consensus concerning binding values, irrevocable standards, and fundamental moral attitudes.[35]

The agreement is careful to state that a global ethic does not mean a global ideology or a single unified religion to replace all existing religions, and it does not call for the domination of one religion over all others. Affirming that without a pervasive global ethic, sooner or later every community will be threatened by chaos or dictatorship, the statement addresses three major areas. The first is the belief that every human being must be treated humanely, that every human being possesses an inalienable and untouchable dignity, and that everyone, other individuals as well as the state, is therefore obligated to honor this dignity and protect it. The second is a group of irrevocable directives committed to a culture of nonviolence and respect for life, a culture of solidarity and a just economic order, a culture of tolerance and a life of truthfulness, and a culture of equal rights and partnership between men and women. The final section speaks to a transformation of consciousness. Citing signs of positive change in areas such as war and peace, economy and ecology, the document calls for the transformation of individuals and society.[36]

At the beginning of this lecture, I described a globe designed from composite photos taken from space that showed no political boundaries. A photograph taken by Rick Darby from a helicopter hovering above the spire of the Temple also shows no political boundaries on the map built into the world plaza. God's Spirit moving in ever expanding circles makes a broken world whole through belief transformed into activity in pursuit of peace. May we find the insight to see our world as its Creator must see it, and may we find the wisdom and the determination to work toward the creation of the universal family that our Creator surely intends for humankind.

## Notes

1. Richard Falk, *A Study of Future Worlds* (New York: The Free Press, 1975), 59ff.
2. James Turner Johnson, *The Quest for Peace: Three Moral Traditions in Western Cultural History* (Princeton, New Jersey: Princeton University Press, 1987), 260.
3. Hedley Bull, "The Idea of International Society", *The Anarchical Society: A Study of Order in World Politics* (New York: Columbia University Press, 1977), 24–27.
4. Julius Stone, *Vision of World Order: Between State Power and Human Justice* (Baltimore, Maryland: Johns Hopkins University Press, 1984), 16.
5. W. Scott Thompson and Kenneth M. Jensen, eds., *Approaches to Peace: An Intellectual Map* (Washington, D.C.: United States Institute of Peace, 1991), 142.
6. Ibid., 154ff.
7. Benjamin B. Ferencz and Ken Keyes, Jr., *Planethood: The Key to Your Future* (Coos Bay, Oregon: Love Line Books, 1991), 11.

8. Keith D. Suter, "The Long Search for Peace," *Alternatives to War*, 2d ed. (Sydney, Australia: Women's International League for Peace and Freedom, 1986), 59–78.
9. Robert Muller, *Dialogues of Hope* (self-published, 1990), 173ff.
10. Barbara Wade Rose, "Keeping The Peace," *Imperial Oil Review 77, no. 409 (Summer 1993), 7ff.*
11. Muller, 51.
12. Glen H. Stassen, *Just Peacemaking: Transforming Initiatives for Justice and Peace* (Louisville, Kentucky: Westminster/John Knox Press, 1992), 138.
13. Ibid.
14. Ibid.
15. Peter Meyer, "How the International Bill of Human Rights Was Born," *The International Bill of Human Rights*, ed. Paul Williams (Glen Ellen, California: Entwhistle Books, 1981); David Krieger and Frank Kelly, *Waging Peace II: Vision and Hope for the 21st Century* (Chicago: The Noble Press,1992), 183ff; Ferencz and Keyes, 66–67.
16. Jimmy Carter, *Talking Peace: A Vision for the Next Generation* (New York: Dutton's Children's Books, 1993), 100.
17. Quoted by Francis Beer, *Peace Against War: The Ecology of International Violence* (San Francisco: W.H. Freeman and Company, 1981), 134–135.
18. Robert Jay Lifton, *History and Human Survival* (New York: Random House, 1961), 231–233.
19. Ibid.
20. Francis Beer.
21. Stephen Covey, *The Seven Habits of Highly Effective People* (New York: Simon & Schuster, 1989), 219–220.
22. Lisbon Statement on Global Interdependence and National Sovereignty, Interaction Council Composed of Former Heads of Governments (March 11, 1991); Ferencz and Keyes, 154.
23. George Mills, "Revisiting Westminster 46 Years Later," *The Kansas City Star* (Saturday, May 9, 1992).
24. Krieger and Kelly, 389.
25. Ibid., 8–9.
26. Grenville Clark and Louis Sohn, *World Peace Through World Law* (Cambridge, Massachusetts: Harvard University Press, 1960).
27. Falk, 174ff.
28. Carl Van Doren, *The Great Rehearsal: The Story of the Making and Ratifying of the Constitution of the United States* (New York: Greenwood Press, 1982).
29. Strobe Talbott, "The Birth of the Global Nation," *Time* (July 20, 1992), 70–71.
30. Falk, 72.

31. Krieger and Kelly, 141.
32. Ferencz and Keyes, 25–27.
33. Elise Boulding, *Building a Global Civic Culture: Education for an Interdependent World* (New York: Teachers College Press, 1988), chapter 3.
34. "Peacebuilding Through Collaborative Action," Institute for Multi-Track Diplomacy, 1133 20th Street NW, Washington, D.C. 20036-3408.
35. "World Parliament of Religions," *The Los Angeles Times* (Sunday, September 5, 1993), A-1.
36. "Toward a Global Ethic," 1993 Parliament of the World's Religions.

# Can We Imagine a World Full of Peace?

A few years ago a young Olympic skier was seriously injured during training for the Winter Games. Her leg required three months of rest to heal so she could ski again. During that time of enforced quiet, she imaged her skiing technique, correcting its weaknesses, practicing, practicing—in her mind. When at last she returned to the slopes, her skill had grown significantly from the level of her pre-accident ability. *The power of imagination!*

It takes an extraordinary act of imagination to recognize and adjust to what Thomas Kuhn calls a "paradigm shift." Kuhn defines a paradigm "as an accepted model or pattern....from which springs a particular coherent tradition." A paradigm shift then is not a small adjustment or a minor revision of an accepted model or pattern but a departure so abrupt and so radical that it destroys the old pattern. Focusing primarily on scientific discovery, Kuhn offers evidence that most researchers are so blinded by existing paradigms they do not even recognize the evidence that does not fit. He describes the great landmark developments in the sciences as such breaks with past knowledge. It is the truly original mind that heeds these departures from the accepted pattern and follows them, often to new and startling breakthroughs in scientific understanding.[1]

Richard Smoke and Willis Harman present evidence that the human imagination is already at work reordering past social models and patterns in radical ways. They call the transformation the opening up of the "new age," a phrase viewed with great suspicion and hostility by some people.[2] Surely the phrase has a distinguished lineage. The Christian era was the "new age," and the book of Revelation speaks of "a new heaven and a new earth." Every period in the world's history has surely been a "bad old age," and the present age has not achieved perfection. So what about this "new age"? Lewis Mumford wrote that Western civilization has experienced two great shifts in orientation: from the classical, Greco-Roman world to the Middle Ages, and from the Middle Ages to the modern world. Mumford projected the next shift:

> Every transformation of man...has rested on a new metaphysical and ideological base; or rather, upon a new picture of the cosmos and the nature of man....We stand on the brink of [such a] new age...an age of renewal...and a higher trajectory for life as a whole....In carrying man's self-transformation to this further stage, world culture may bring about a fresh release of spiritual energy that will unveil new potentialities, no more visible in the human self today than radium was in the physical world a century ago, though always present.[3]

Smoke and Harman list five social trends they believe have set the stage for this transformation: (1) a search for wholeness; (2) a search for community and relationship; (3) a search for identity; (4) a search for meaning; and (5) a search for empowerment.[4] These are recognizable objectives in many of the institutions that employ us; in many cultural movements, some of which have been mentioned in these lectures; and in the recent message and materials from the church. Many contemporary practices are being judged by a new standard based on these five values. Further, there is a basic change in the epistemological roots of many sciences. Physics, for example, has been steadily moving away from its materialistic base to an emphasis on process. In the biological and human sciences a similar change is occurring. Nobel laureate Roger Sperry, writing about ten years ago, called attention to

> recent changes in concepts relating to the mind of man, the nature of the conscious self, freedom of choice, causal determinism and....the fundamental relation of mind to matter and to brain mechanism....Current concepts of the mind-brain relation involve a direct break with the long-established materialist and behaviorist doctrine that has dominated neuroscience for many decades.[5]

Werner Heisenberg, the late Nobel physicist, noted: "In the beginning was the symmetry. That is certainly more correct than Democritus' theory: 'In the beginning was the particle.' The elementary particles incorporate the symmetries; they are their simple representations but they are first a consequence of the symmetries."[6] Surveys of physical, biological, and social sciences reveal similar changes "from structure to process, from linear to multidimensional logic, from mechanistic to holographic models, from hierarchical to nonhierarchical ordering, from a focus on elements to one on 'whole systems,' and most generally from an orientation toward matter-energy to one emphasizing relationships and connections."[7]

In light of these provocative observations, the question raised by the title of this lecture is not an idle or romantic one even though it is a line from an old ballad, "Can we imagine a world full of peace?" If enough of us can imagine a world full of peace, we would truly be part of a paradigm shift more radical and revolutionary than any the world has experienced before in its history. In earlier lectures we have reviewed a number of social and religious paradigms that govern our lives and have observed that they may be inadequate to respond to the historical reality of the closing years of the twentieth century. What are some of those discrepancies?

1. The world's great religions preach peace and practice war.

2. The world's superpowers arm for war to maintain peace.

3. Non-violent resistance as a means of achieving peace is ignored even though its record shows it absorbs hate and hostility, turning it into shame and the desire to repent on the part of the aggressor.

4. In the United States we used to have a secretary of war; we now have a secretary of defense, but we have never had a secretary of peace—for that matter we have four military academies, but no comparable peace academy.

5. Beset by global problems, nations follow self-defeating habits governed by national interests instead of being motivated by the best interest of all human beings.

6. Humankind yearns to be loved and to belong in community but practices hate and distrusts intimacy.

And the list goes on and on.

To achieve a paradigm shift that would incorporate the positive values mentioned above, a critical mass of people would have to come imaginatively to a belief in the possibility of peace through images and symbols, and would have to figure out how to achieve peace through the power of the human intellect. Then these people would be free to pursue peace in the ways that their own creativity suggests. To free the human mind through positive intellectual content is the task of education; to free the human imagination through the images of peace is the task of religion. Religion and education converge in the capacity of reconstruction, cited by E. J. Gleazer, Jr., in a paper prepared for the peace studies committee at Graceland College. Quoting Betty Reardon, he calls attention to the components of the capacity for reconstruction. The first component of the imagination that permits reconstruction is *envisioning*, which enables people to experience insight into the full range of possibilities for realizing human potential through the expression of the most fundamental human values. The second component is *imaging*, which is the visualization and communication of the conditions that would prevail if human ideas were realized. And the third component is *modeling*, the most practical of the three, which includes skills and social and political design.[8]

"Thinking is the urgent work of a species that has responsibility for its survival," wrote Hannah Arendt,[9] thus underlining the importance of the field of peace education and research, both of which have grown tremendously in the past few years. The distinguished Swiss educator Maria Montessori noted: "Establishing lasting peace is the work of education. All politics can do is keep us out of war."[10] Although Montessori would find little disagreement with her position, Carolyn Stephenson notes that "in comparison with the amount of research on most other subjects, including especially the conduct of war and the maintenance of international security,...the amount of research on peace, whether measured in number of researchers or in dollars of research expenditure, has been infinitesimally small."[11] The opponents of peace studies—and there are many—maintain that peace studies cannot be objective and that the real motivation is not academic but rather political and ideological. That argument is akin to saying that the biologist who searches for a cure for cancer is motivated not by objective academic interest but by the humanitarian desire to alleviate suffering, and therefore cannot do valid research. Peace education is attempting to find a respected place among the recognized disciplines into which human knowledge has been divided. Beginning with the decade between 1960 and 1970 and drawing from many existing disciplines, peace studies has developed a theoretical and a knowledge base, the two elements that entitle it to a place in the panoply of legitimate academic disciplines.[12]

Many institutions are including peace education and peace research in their mission or have been organized for that specific purpose. In 1969, U Thant, then secretary-general of the United Nations, proposed that an international university be established for the purpose of gathering scholars to work on the "pressing global problems of human survival, development and welfare." A sweeping mandate called for study of the coexistence between peoples of different cultures, languages, and social systems; peaceful relations between states and the maintenance of peace and security; human rights; economic and social change and development; scientific research and the application of the results of science and technology; and universal human values related to the improvement of the quality of life. Unfortunately, fiscal resources have never matched this mandate. Its headquarters are now located in Costa Rica, and it is led by the distinguished diplomat, Robert Muller, who works tirelessly to promote it and to gather the finances to further its mission.[13]

Better funded is the United States Institute of Peace. Created in 1984 by Congress, the institute's objective was to establish an undergraduate peace academy as a counterpart to the military academies. Although it does not enroll traditional students, grant degrees, or lobby for specific policies, and although its financial support is not comparable, it has sponsored conferences and funded research projects that relate to the search for peace. Among its accomplishments are the following: hundreds of manuscripts, books, articles, and reports produced by distinguished international scholars, diplomats, and other experts; expert working groups organized to probe options for peacemaking in the wake of fast-breaking international events; educational materials for classroom and curriculum enrichment, teacher training workshops, and video packages for classroom use and educational television; technical assistance for people directly involved in drafting new constitutions, teaching mediation, and negotiating peace agreements; and development of a national library network, data bases, and services linking libraries across the country.[14]

In an attempt to grasp the full scope of the field of peace studies, the institute in the winter of 1986–1987 began the formal structuring of its Intellectual Map Project. Scholars developed a topology on which to base the conceptual organization of the study of international conflict and peacemaking. This map divides the study of warmaking and peacemaking into four major categories: (1) a study of the traditional approaches, which include attention to collective security and deterrence, diplomacy and negotiation, and strategic management and arms control; (2) a study of legal approaches, which include international law, interstate organizations, and third-party dispute settlement; (3) a study of new approaches, which include transnationalism, behavioral knowledge, and conflict resolution; and (4) a study of political systems approaches, which include internal systems, systemic theories, and world systems.[15]

Many colleges are incorporating peace majors and minors or areas of concentration into existing curricula. These efforts are usually interdisciplinary and attempt to bring together the best knowledge available. The field is enormous and is beginning to achieve a distinguished reputation. Even though career opportunities are not numerous, students are interested in the subject and are choosing to spend precious college time studying it.

Religion teaches values and encourages behavior consistent with them. It attempts to inspire people to rise above their limitations to live a life that is better than it might otherwise have been. In a 1932 letter responding to Albert Einstein's desire to know if psychology held any answer to the problem of armament, aggression, or war, Sigmund Freud repeated his thesis that human personality is divided between love and aggression. "The attainment of peace therefore requires the development of all possible means, of ties of feeling and love among human beings. It is necessary to create common objectives and sentiments which bind the human family. The love of country has succeeded in binding people at the national level. The great, new historic challenge is to develop ties of feeling and love among all Earth's inhabitants and for the planet itself."[16] Thomas Merton observed:

> If we can love the men we cannot trust (without trusting them foolishly) and if we can to some extent share the burden of their sin by identifying ourselves with them, then perhaps there is some hope for a kind of peace on earth, based not on the wisdom and the manipulations of men but on the inscrutable mercy of God.[17]

The world's great religions all proclaim brotherhood and empathy for other human beings. The great religious symbols of peace and brotherhood inspire individuals to rise above their inherent natural or socialized meanness and develop a spiritual maturity that approximates the ideals held up by religious teaching. Human beings have demonstrated that they have the capacity to expand their consciousness to include other human beings. If we can do so for family and nation, why not for the world?[18] Gordon Kaufman notes that religion "with its concern for mythic consciousness, the religious imagination and human hope and despair"[19] is uniquely suited to deal with the spiritual dimensions of the paradigm shift.

Religion must be very careful what it teaches. Most of us would feel uncomfortable today with the military imagery of some of the old hymns. "God is Marshaling His Army" and "Onward Christian Soldiers" do not have a place in the peace hymnal. I was surprised to learn recently, however, from a five-year-old friend that his children's choir was singing, "I may never march with the infantry, ride with the cavalry, shoot with artillery, I may never fly over Germany, but I'm in the Lord's army." I don't know how he deals with the World War II imagery—and perhaps there is a peace message in there somewhere—but I doubt very much that it reaches him.

(He would fly anywhere if he had the chance, and I am sorry to report that he shoots with an impressive array of make-believe artillery in his neighborhood play.) I trust that this selection is a singular hold-over from an earlier time. The material and mood of the church now is much different.

Any discussion of education and religion must be careful not to compartmentalize these two domains. That compartmentalization of the rational and the spiritual is one of the old paradigms. Education and religion should be part of a whole. Bernard Haring observed: "A concept of faith broadened to include response and active responsibility on all levels depends upon a conception of revelation broadened to include the whole of accessible knowledge about man and the world."[20] Sections 85, 87, and 90 of the Doctrine and Covenants express that vision of wholeness even more clearly, identifying all knowledge as the raw material of prophetic behavior.

In a thoughtful analysis of the "Core Values of the RLDS Church," Anthony Chvala-Smith identified one pattern of meaning in the RLDS tradition as "the expectation of new things." He quoted Jurgen Moltmann who wrote: "Meaningful action is always possible only within a horizon of expectation, otherwise all...actions would be desperate thrusts into a void...."[21] The enthusiastic and creative response of members of the RLDS Church to the challenge to pursue peace is indeed "meaningful action with expectations." Remarkable institutional and individual initiatives have attempted to find ways to inspire the efforts of a wide variety of people and to help them develop their own definition of peacemaking and discover their own ways of pursuing it. This effort preceded 1984, when Section 156 provided an authoritative focus.

In addition to World Conference resolutions, many other pioneering activities prepared the way for Section 156. Since 1984 many new initiatives have been developed by individuals and groups.

A project sponsored by the North Atlantic States Region targets the Aaronic priesthood office of teacher but invites all people interested in peace and reconciliation ministries to participate. The *Newsletter*, dedicated to the pursuit of peace, is informing its readers about the resources available to teach peaceful conflict management to children and adults. The Aaronic Teacher Network is committed to exploring new horizons in peacemaking, conflict resolution, and reconciliation ministries in congregations, branches, and missions. Galen Worthington, holding a master's degree in conflict resolution, is developing the training materials for conflict management.

Two examples of individual initiative are the newly organized PeaceForum and the Young Peacemakers Club. Diane Kyser and Randall Pratt have developed an organization and a newsletter whose mission is "to empower persons to share ideas and enthusaism for the pursuit of peace, to live as peacemakers, and to express our identity as a faith community of peace." The PeaceForum is independent of the church and will attempt to accomplish its mission through the publication of newsletters, journals, and other materials to creatively explore ideas related to peace. The organization will feature essays, poetry, music, reports on projects; create educational materials and opportunities; organize local chapters in various geographic areas for study and networking with the local community; and sponsor conferences, retreats, and other events.

Kelly Guinan of Sioux City, Iowa, has developed the Young Peacemakers Club concept, which is attracting significant attention in her locale and throughout the church. A nonsectarian effort for children in second through fifth grades, its purpose is to introduce and/or deepen children's relationships to the teachings and person of Jesus Christ as Prince of Peace; to guide children in experiential learning and present expressions of inner peace, relational peace, world peace, and environmental peace; to empower children in their desire and their skill development for acts of peacemaking and social service; and to foster intercultural and interracial understanding and acceptance in the community. Kelly's work has been featured by the media in her area; seven clubs now exist in Sioux City, and the concept, without explicit religious reference, has been invited into the public schools. Kelly also has been invited to many church jurisdictions to explain the concept. In October 1993 a community celebration of peace and unity planned by Guinan and sponsored by the Young Peacemaker's Clubs in Sioux City, attracted 1,500 kite-flying participants to the campus of a local college. Called "One Sky, One World," it offered sand volleyball, drama, chalk drawing, bubble making, face painting, and, most important, an opportunity for different races and ages to gather in celebration. Modest funding from Tangible Love and Kelly's generous donation of her own time and creativity have supported the Young Peacemaker's Clubs thus far. Not only does the idea promise to have a significant impact on the lives of young people, but it already has resulted in baptisms as its connection with the church becomes known.

These examples represent the many ways individuals and congregations are feeding the hungry, intervening in conflict, protecting the environment, supporting human rights, and imaging peace. Church members have heard the call to be agents of transformation in the world. Can it be that the institution that once thought of itself as the exclusive representative of God in the world—the "one true church"—in becoming committed to the pursuit of peace has found a new calling as it engages in the pursuit of peace? Can it be that we as an institution and as individuals have for our time recognized the purpose of God's Spirit at work in the world and have joined it in its saving work? If we do not risk moving beyond what we have understood in the past to be our identity, then we run an even greater risk of becoming irrelevant to our members and to the world. In our pursuit of peace we can become a prophetic minority for our time.

The Temple Peace Center is an important institutional response to the challenge to pursue peace. The major emphases of Christ's ministry provide direction for the concept of Temple ministry. Education, service, abundant life, worship, proclamation,and peace are the central ideas around which the ministry of the Temple is organized. Each of these tasks can be seen as related intimately to the pursuit of peace. Thus the Temple Peace Center is only one of the foci of Temple ministry charged with the task of helping church members find ways to pursue peace.

The mission statement of the Temple Peace Center addresses its mandate directly: *The Temple Peace Center responds to God by helping people envision and create a more just, compassionate, and peaceful world.* All of the activities of the center are tested by that statement. The Children's Peace Pavilion reflects the belief that teaching peace to children is primary. This interactive museum is being developed under the leadership of Marla Blevins and a dedicated group of specialists in chlidhood education. I invite you to walk with me through the pavilion:

We begin in the theater where elementary-school children will view a video that helps them understand some of the components of peace and introduces them to the experiences that will follow. In small groups they will walk through the tunnel connecting the Temple to the Auditorium. Panels of brightly colored carpet on the wall will provide background for children's artwork depicting their visions of peace. A mural prepared by one of the classes at the 1993 International Youth Forum also will be on display there. On reaching the Auditorium, the children will go to the former museum where twenty-five to thirty exhibits will help them act out experiences of inner peace, peace in their relationships with family and friends, peace in the world, and peace with the environment. Entering a large shell, the child will have the feeling of being under water and can sit quietly for a few minutes listening to sea sounds and looking at rainbows of light. Children will play an interactive video game that explores different emotions and how to acknowledge and use them productively. They will explore cooperative activities that require synergy between participants, such as a light and sound game in which small groups can make music together by stepping on specific spots on the floor. An international post office will take a message from the child to a child in another country, translate it into the appropriate language, and send it off. Dolls in native dress will be matched with language and geographic location. A conflict resolution theater will provide models of successful conflict behavior through puppets and role playing. The child will have a picture taken with a large lion and lamb, and that picture will become part of a peace passport that identifies the child as a member of the global community. Then the children will go back through the tunnel and into the double classroom on the east side of the Temple where the child will become a Young Peacemaker through several crafts and games. The pavilion is designed for families with elementary-age children to experience the activities together and for public school class field trips. Pre- and post-visit packets of materials for classroom activities will enhance the educational value.

The Peace Colloquy is an annual event in which an internationally recognized peacemaker will be honored with a $25,000 award to be contributed to a peacemaking activity. The weekend will address a substantive peace issue and will attract people from many religious faiths. In December 1993, Jehan Sadat was honored for her humanitarian work in Egypt. At her request the award was contributed to the Anwar Sadat Chair of Population, Development and Peace at the University of Maryland, which honors her late husband. The 1993 colloquy featured an interfaith gathering of Muslims, Jews, and Christians that discussed the resources for peace found in each of the three faiths. Conferees shared their peacemaking activities. An interfaith musical celebration of diversity and an interfaith worship service provided added dimensions of understanding and appreciation. An original drama by John Horner defining peace was presented. Each year by its very nature the colloquy will communicate to the community and to the church that the Temple's ministry will bring together many people who share a common concern for peacemaking.

Another Peace Center project, Peaceworks, will be presented as part of the Temple visit program. A series of videos will hold up a variety of peace issues from inner peace to international conflict. Facilitators will lead discussions on issues, and further reading and investigation will be recommended. The objective of this activity is to stimulate thinking about what peace is and how individuals can engage in its pursuit.

The Temple Peace Center also is participating with other peace organizations whose missions are compatible locally, nationally, and internationally. Combining its influence with that of other organizations to impact the problems that face human beings allows us to expand our efforts and enhance theirs and gives us opportunities to witness our commitment.

So we return to the point at which we began these lectures. What is peace and how can we, who are motivated by the Christian gospel of peace, pursue it? Finally, each of us and the church must answer these two questions for ourselves. The New Testament does not provide us with a final definition or a set of specific instructions. What we do have is the story of how one person and his followers pursued peace in their day and time, a time so unlike ours that it is only the principles that are relevant for us and our world. What we must seek is the living word of God for today, which the RLDS Church in its best moments has always done, which word will have the power to move us, change us, and inspire us.

The task is enormous and we are a small church, but we do not act alone. People of spiritual insight all over the world are responding to the imperative for peace in unprecedented numbers, and their efforts are making a difference. Most important, we do not act alone because the Spirit of God precedes us and shows us the way if we have eyes to see. Do we dare believe that it is the pursuit of peace that can have the unifying power to bring together people of goodwill, wherever they dwell, whatever language they speak, and whatever or whomever they call God? Remembering the words of Ephesians 2:14, spoken also to small congregations and isolated individuals scattered throughout the world, may we resolve to go forth to do the work of peace wherever we have opportunity:

> For Christ himself has brought us peace by making all the peoples of the world one people. With his own body he broke down the wall that separated them and kept them enemies....in order to create out of the races of the world one new people in union with himself, in this way making peace. By his death on the cross Christ destroyed their enmity; by means of the cross he united all races into one body and brought them back to God. So Christ came and preached the Good News of peace to all—to those who were far away from God, and to those who were near to him. It is through Christ that all of us are able to come in one Spirit into the presence of the Creator.

## Notes

1. Thomas Kuhn, *The Structure of Scientific Revolution* (Chicago: University of Chicago Press, 1970), 10.
2. Richard Smoke and Willis Harmon, "Paths to Peace," in *Dilemmas of War and Peace: A Source Book*, Dick Ringler, ed. (Board of Regents of the University of Wisconsin System and the Corporation for Public Broadcasting, 1993), 195–197.
3. Lewis Mumford, *The Transformation of Man* (New York: Harper, 1956).
4. Smoke and Harmon.

5. Quoted by W. Scott Thompson and Kenneth M. Jensen, eds., *Approaches to Peace: An Intellectual Map* (United States Institute of Peace, 1991), 246.
6. Jurgen Moltmann, *Creating a Just Future: The Politics of Peace and the Ethics of Creation in a Threatened World* (Philadelphia: Trinity Press International, 1989), 68.
7. Smoke and Harmon.
8. E. J. Gleazer, Jr., "A Report for Use in Preparing a Peace Studies Curriculum" (n.p.: 1988), 13–14.
9. Hannah Arendt, *On Violence* (New York: Harcourt, Brace & World, 1969), 279.
10. Colman McCarthy, "Peace Education: The Time Is Now," *The Washington Post* (Tuesday, December 19, 1992).
11. Carolyn Stevenson, "A Research Agenda on the Conditions of Peace," *Exploratory Project on the Conditions of Peace*, The Ex Pro Papers 37 (1987), 3–6.
12. Peace Research Achievements and Challenges, Peter Wallensteen, ed. (Boulder, Colorado: Westview Press, 1988).
13. *The United Nations University* (U.N. Publication, 1988).
14. *Biennial Report of the United States Institute of Peace, 1991*, viii–ix.
15. Ibid.
16. Quoted in Robert Muller, *New Genesis: Shaping a Global Spirituality* (Garden City, New York: Doubleday & Company, 1982), xv.
17. Thomas Merton, *Seeds of Contemplation* (New York: New Directions, 1972), 119.
18. Julius Stone, *Vision of World Order: Between State Power and Human Justice* (Baltimore, Maryland: The Johns Hopkins University Press, 1984).
19. Gordon Kaufman, 38.
20. Quoted in *Theology and Church in Times of Change*, Edward LeRoy Long, Jr., and Robert T. Handy, eds., (Philadelphia: The Westminster Press, 1975), 58.
21. This previously unpublished paper written for Vision 2000 is now available as a booklet in the *Congregational Leaders Handbook* (Independence, Missouri: Herald Publishing House, 1994).